SOUL LIGHT

Solutions for Embracing Life's Challenges and Living a Life You Love

MANDI MILLER

SOUL LIGHT

Solutions for Embracing Life's Challenges and Living a
Life You Love

MANDI MILLER

INDYROX Publishing

Contents

Dedication

I am dedicating this book to my kids, Indy and Roxanne. I was born to be your Mama and you have completed my soul. Thank you for all your endless love, and support and laughs. You two really are the best! My God we are a lucky bunch!

My muse Markcos, thank you for teaching me more about myself than anyone else, and you always believe in me. I am so grateful. We definitely live life in color! Love you.

My parents. Mom and Dad, thank you for having me. I wouldn't be who I am nor would I be brave enough to share who I am if it wasn't for your unconditional love. Dad you have always encouraged my true potential, thank you for all your love and support. And mom thanks for sending me all the hearts.

Introduction

Who am I? What qualifies me to be giving anyone else advice?

When I was 15, while on a family vacation, my mother and I were in a horrific crash a drunk driver smashed into us. I survived. My mom did not. She died instantly. The life I knew, the life I had, the life I thought I would have had all changed forever.

Through my resilience and strength and having to find faith over and over again, I taught myself to forgive. I taught myself how to create the life I wanted, dreamed of, and deserved.

I have been through hell and back many, many times. Some situations were not asked for and other times I completely take full responsibility for the journey. If self-sabotage was an art form I could have been called Picasso. Happily, I have learned many lessons now on how to avoid such toxic behaviours and attitudes towards myself. Ultimately, I know I'm the only person I have control over.

I have lost a lot of soulmates along the way on my journey from illnesses, suicide, a drug overdose, and Alzheimer's. I myself am a cancer survivor and refuse to ever give up, give in or quit.

I have also gained and made the best memories and friend-ships and experiences that life can possibly offer. I am surrounded by an army of incredible souls. The lack of family at times, made me have to create my own, and I chose wisely the souls that to this day are my family. My safe space, my support, love, adventure seekers and comedians that help keep my heart light and keep my life amazing! And happily, my blood family has overcome many obstacles to find a place of peace together and so much love.

I've learned the art of perspective and the importance of being in the moment now, not just talking about it, but living it. Self-love, acceptance, forgiveness, insight, vision, moving forward and so many more life tools that we need in our tool boxes is what this book and these words are about.

It's not just finding the light in the dark but feeling it. I want you to know you are never truly alone. We are guided by our spirit and connected by our souls.

It is time to let go of the labels and expectations. It's now the time to love and move on and forward without judgement. I want you to take yourself on a journey of discovery and forgiveness, creating a calmer, easier experience no matter what life throws at you. Realize your own part and responsi-bility in your experiences. Even when shit happens and it's not good, it's bad and you don't like it or welcome it, well then, it's time to shift your thoughts and the way you are thinking. Turn your perspective around and make it a better situation.

Shit is always going to happen! This is life. This is living! But you are the only one who chooses how much power you give it. That is the beauty of our souls and minds and hearts. We have the power and the choice in every situation as to what we choose to do with it.

I believe we are here experiencing all the lessons and blessings that our souls need to be able to become more enlightened.

With our souls becoming more enlightened comes the ability for ourselves to reach our highest and best use here on earth.

I don't believe we started here, and I don't believe we end here. I believe we arrived and will inevitably return back home when this adventure has come to an end. And then we begin a new adventure and continue on.

We are always searching. Searching for answers. Searching for meaning. Searching for our soul's purpose. I am here to tell you that you already have all the answers and they have always been there inside of you. It takes courage to open up, to sometimes admit the things you would rather not admit to. But it's all OK! Don't ever fear change and the beauty that you deserve! You are here for a reason! Now let's get started! Have some fun and go on an adventure!

I made a promise to myself thirty-two years ago that I would make sure I share with people what life has taught me. Through my lessons, my hope is to not only help other people, but to inspire and remind you how precious you are. My wish is that after you read Soul Light, that you feel Soul Light. Make this life what you want it to be. Feel how you wish to feel. Do what you need to do to make your journey incredible. Its always been up to you.

ONE

Are You Shining as Bright as You Can?

UNDERSTANDING HOW AND WHEN YOU NEED A
CHANGE

Do you ever feel like you are losing touch with yourself?

You know what's going on inside but at the same time feel disconnected from your core. This is the perfect time to reconnect, get back in touch, maybe become more inspired.

But how?

Nature is an amazing abundance of positive energy. Every blade of grass is life. The trees, leaves, flowers, sky, dirt; all contain endless amounts of positive energy.

Think about the process plants have to go through just to grow. What a miracle! We are no different, our process began the moment our cells started to multiply.

If you can't go outside and just be, simply sit by a window or a plant and observe. Breathe, be still, and become grounded to the earth again. Feel the connection. Feel the energy and good vibrations. Allow yourself to let go of anything holding you down and just be. This can help you reconnect within yourself once again. Feeling the ever positive and growing energy of the natural environment around us.

Do you listen to your inner voice?

When there is someone on your mind and you keep thinking about them, maybe that is a sign that you should reach out to them.

Thinking about someone constantly or they keep popping up in your thoughts, maybe things keep reminding you of them is all part of your inner self and invisible guides telling you something. I've heard many times that ninety percent of the time when you are thinking about somebody it is because they are thinking about you. It's an interesting thought.

It might not even be about you but maybe this person in your thoughts; they need to hear from you. Maybe they need your energy in this moment. Your loving spirit needs to be shared.

Never dismiss the power of your spirit and inner self when it is trying to get your attention. This is exactly when it is not only so important to pay attention but take the next step and act on it. Trust yourself and listen to your heart. It is always speaking to you. This also applies to everything not just when thinking about others, but your heart is your biggest guide to whether you are on the right track in life or not. If it doesn't feel right, pay attention. Things need to feel right by you in order to guide you to where it is your journey wants you to go.

Do you listen to your gut feelings?

Everybody has a certain degree of intuition or aka 'Spidey senses.' Do you often pay attention to your gut or feeling that you sometimes get or not?

Some people are very tuned into their intuition and use it to guide a lot of what they do or don't do. They feel the situation and people around them. They are open to vibrations coming from all around. They are listening to their inner voice.

Other people don't believe in such non-sense. They are closed off to the idea that we can use our grandest perceptions to help guide us through life and moments. And maybe just go with the facts in the mind, not the heart or soul.

We do posses a part of our brains that drives the insights we can't see or be told.

But within ourselves, feel it. Know it and go with it. Ignoring the gut feeling can possibly take you places on your path like a detour that you really didn't have time for or a need for. Listen to yourself and trust yourself. The more you practise this the easier it becomes, and the smoother life gets.

Do you ever wish or pray or dream of a way out of a situation?

Just to hear the cliché, "There's no way out, just through." Well, what does that mean? I believe that yes you must go "through" in order to get "out", but is there a right or wrong way to do it? There are probably ways less harmful or more productive to get out of and through a situation for sure.

In the moment we are always making decisions that create our future. Looking back at past situations whether it's a friend-ship or work, love, family, or any type of life's interesting, momentous predicaments we find ourselves in; it's the way we get through that has the outcome attached. We can't always predict everything or anyone's reactions to our decisions or our own reactions. So, what do we do?

You, me, we all do the very best we can in that moment with what we have. Maybe hindsight will tell you differently one day but making decisions with our best intentions and trying to minimize any hurt or suffering should be paramount. Then when you look back at it, whether you agree with your past decisions on how you handled it, when you know that in your heart you did the best you could with your best intentions, you should feel okay about it. And who can blame you for that?

Are you getting in the way of yourself?

Are you a self-saboteur? Maybe your inside head voice is negative and mean and judgmental, always thinking the worst. Maybe it continually is thinking way ahead of any situation and expecting the worst will happen.

If you notice yourself doing this, and you constantly go to these dark places and spaces then that would be the first step in changing this toxic behaviour. It's the beginning of shifting the script. If you notice you do this, instantly stop yourself. Take a look around you in real time and find a positive physical thing to focus on, like a pretty or loving picture, a plant, the sky, open a door or window stick your head out and smell the fresh air. Find something in that moment and shift your attention.

Your mind will take a break and begin to recharge.

Switching your thoughts quickly, and to become in the moment rather than in a place you are not yet there like the future is the goal. Exercise your inner voice to stop judging or justifying negative thoughts and behaviors that are harmful. Tell yourself enough! Look around in the moment and be thankful. Be thankful for your breath if there's nothing else you can see. Be thankful for what is in front of you and what you do have.

Do you blame yourself for things that have happened that were not controlled by you?

What if.........

What if I had done this instead of that? What if I made a different decision or choice in that moment? What if I was one minute earlier? What if I was one minute later?

The what if game can go on indefinitely your whole life. But it isn't necessary or productive. It can actually and probably will make you crazy. If it's past it's gone, out of reach no matter how much you dwell on it.

The only what-if moments that are good for us are the fun ones. Like how cool chance encounters are, meeting kindred spirits or witnessing a miracle. Being in the right place at the right time.

What if in retrospect there's nothing that should be changed, good and bad, even if you could change it. Because the truth is, you wouldn't be who you are today without all your experiences and moments from yesterday. Trust this and trust yourself, just the way you are. We only can control so much of our lives and can't blame ourselves for the things that happen beyond our control. No one knows if things that happen are meant to be like a grand design or plan playing out or if life really is just a game of chance. But I do know that no matter which it is, we must make the best of it. Ask yourself: how can

I learn and grow from this? It's the only way to live. Find the light in the dark.

What is control? Is it the same as power? Does it equal power?

The dictionary defines control like this: "the power to influence or direct people's behavior or the course of events." As a verb, control means: "to be in charge."

What happens to us when we feel we don't have any control? So often life happens beyond our control, and we then must decide how to deal with and react to situations beyond our control. Or we don't decide we just react without any sense of control. Because we have already lost our sense of control instantly.

What about self-control? We all must possess some degree of it or else the world would be completely feral. But every so often we lose it. Or we find out we actually don't have it. Or we give it up, especially to others. Usually, when we feel powerless is the time we lose our self-control. Trying to be in charge of a situation and it's not happening the way we want it to play out can go very sideways very fast. We grasp at anything sometimes to feel like we still have power in the situation. We must be gentle with ourselves and use our control of ourselves to do good. Suggesting positivity instead of trying to force it and breathe before reacting. It's okay to delay any response. Taking the time to think about reactions is always valuable. This shows restraint and control of ourselves. Slowing down the response time is wise, and letting things go organically the way they will is also a blessing. And there may even be times where we need to surrender to a situation, wave the white flag so to speak.

So, maybe to be in control is to be able to let go while maintaining self control, in which then it comes back to the fact that we have control and the power. We don't have to control everything around us, but we do best if we can control our selves to some degree and our emotions.

Are you open to receiving?

Receive love, attention, gifts, friendships, relationships, good news, good health, a good life? Are you ready to receive?

Think about that for a moment. Maybe part of us is shut down. Deep down inside, we feel we don't deserve the best life has to give us.

If this rings true with you, then it's time to change these unhealthy, untrue thoughts. You do absolutely deserve all the good out there coming your way!

Start by believing life can change for you. It's all there waiting for you to accept it. When you manifest good feelings with your thoughts and believe it's your turn, then be ready to receive. Feel right now what it will feel like and recognize as you begin to get the things you asked for. Don't reject the love, attention, gifts, good news, the job, the health, money, and relationships. Be open to all the possibilities that do get sent your way.

I know that there was a time in my life that I didn't even realize I was getting everything I wanted. I was so consumed with bitterness and anger over past events and issues long gone, that I neglected the wonderfulness happening all around me. I felt so ripped off and pissed off about whatever crap I had gone through that that was all I began to expect from life. I attracted crappy people and created crappy moments to actually subconsciously mirror my bad attitude. I felt the world had judged me and it had made up its mind on the path I was to take. Now, that is total bullshit! I am so happy that somehow, I persevered and got my head out of my ass. Life is always offering you what you ask for, so be open to it. Be open to receiving all the wonderful gifts of beauty around you. Be willing to accept that good things are meant for you.

How well do you handle unexpected changes?

Flexibility. How flexible do you think you are, not physically but in general in your mind, in life? When you have things planned a certain way, expect them to happen a certain way and say something disrupts things, how do you handle it?

The thing is that everyday unexpected things are occurring. Unplanned situations pop up. Do you spend the rest of your day upset by this or do you move on quickly, adapt and adjust to the new situation? Of course, I am talking in this sense about the more trivial day-to-day adventures, but it does also hold court with the big stuff we go through too, just on a much different scale and timeline.

Realizing when there's nothing you can do about sudden, unexpected changes to situations try to see them through with anticipation, excitement that the universe is putting you in a different place. Cheer up, it's never the end of the world when changes happen. It's just different than expected. Adapt to your new direction and enjoy the journey! Get on with it!

Are you searching for a place where you belong?

I really don't fit in anywhere. I've tried and searched my whole life to find my place where I belong, but I just never seemed to fit the spot. I struggled for years to try and fit into places, groups, people. It took me a long time to figure out that the most important place I needed to fit into was my own self acceptance. Forget any judgments people put on me, learning to not care about what others thought of me, dropping unwanted expectations of me, and to stop comparing myself to others.

What if you are not meant to fit, maybe you were born to break all the molds that already exist. All your life and experiences have led you to a place that you need to create, that spot you crave to fit into.

Maybe there are others also searching for a similar space to fit in and they are unaware that it's you they are waiting for. You create this space designed for you. Your own unique place that maybe isn't just for you but others as well that feel the same way.

You need to create this reality exactly where you want and need to be. You don't have to have all the answers at once. Just knowing you are here and have arrived is enough. Start believing now that you can be who you are.

The only place that you actually need to fit into is yourself. Your heart, mind and soul should accept your true self, flaws and all. That is where we all belong. Because once we learn our space is our own unique place in this world, so will everyone else! And there truly is nothing more flattering or attractive than people who have the confidence to just be themselves without a care in the world, fitting in with others or not. When we carry that feeling of being comfortable with ourselves, then things seem to fall into place. The right feelings, the right people who are similar to us, we find our places when we accept our differences from other people and realize the world needs all of our uniqueness we are blessed with. It would be silly to expect a kiwi to become a banana, right? It just isn't possible. We need the kiwi to be just the way it is, and we need the banana to stay exactly as the banana is, sweet and delicious!

Are you afraid of failing?

I remember at one time in my life I told someone that my biggest fear was failing. I was afraid to fail above all other things.

When I think back to when I made those statements, I can appreciate who I was, and what circumstances were surrounding me at that time. I know exactly where I was in that moment.

I whole-heartedly disagree with past Mandi now on those old beliefs. What life has taught me in the fourteen years since claiming those thoughts is in actuality I shouldn't fear failing.

There is no such thing as failing or being a failure at something. It's just not true. Instead, there are situations that may not work out the way we pictured them to or hoped they would. Maybe there were moments where we didn't do the 'right' thing. Decisions we may have made that could have had a better route instead of the path we chose in the moment. So, you could have made better choices at times perhaps. But, but, but... Do not ever dismiss where you were in your head, heart and soul when you were making these choices. Your surroundings were probably very different than what you see around you now.

Maybe you're dealing with fallout right now from bad decision making. That's okay. You're not a failure because of it, your human. And you are learning and growing because of these lessons. This wakes us up. This stirs our core when we have to pick up the pieces. This is life!

Messy, ugly, sad, disappointing sometimes. This is where we root down and grow upwards from. You have not failed. You have lived. You are taking a path that is new and different from the direction you may have imagined. But that does not mean you have failed; you just are going somewhere you didn't antic-ipate. So, buckle up and see things in a different way.

Do you feel like you're running out of time?

I think one of the biggest and hardest thoughts we may have is running out of time. The thought of no longer having the choice to do what maybe we set out to do in the beginning of our journey in life. Leaving things unfinished, incomplete.

It is not a morbid thought to think about when we die. It is a part of life. The only guarantee for certain in life is our own death. We all die. We usually don't know the details in advance, but in the case of a terminal illness we do.

Fear is natural and expected. Facing what scares us deep down and stepping up to it, then getting on with it, that's what you need to do. Do it on your own terms so you can be where you want to be. The dreams you have been waiting for? Go for them. Think about that for a moment. What have you always known is inside you wanting to get out?

We need to take charge while we can. Before there may be a definite timeline. We are truthfully all on an invisible timeline anyway.

Enough sitting on the sidelines and just watching time go by. You know what you desire. Get going on it. Follow up with actions and thoughts towards these things. Get your momentum building and let it move you and the mountains you thought were in the way.

After being diagnosed with cancer and living through the hell and fear of my own mortality, it made me realize there is no time like the present. I survived a fatal car crash, only later to have to deal with cancer. Having to stare death in the face for the second time in my life, it was like another wake up call. If surviving a fatal car crash wasn't enough, it took a cancer diagnosis to really kick my ass into gear. I then must live the life I want and dream of for real, not just in my thoughts and mind. Time to move on it! We are the only thing in our own way, and we are the only person that can make what we want to out of ourselves.

Have you ever had a time when you had to make a decision and were torn between what other people wanted and what you felt in your heart was right?

When these moments happen, in the moment the temporary fix could be one of peace keeping or people pleasing. It might make it okay for a minute but there will be long term effects. And they may be debilitating. You will naturally replay that moment and choice over and over again in your mind.

You knew your decision in you gut and heart was already made. And you won't ever forget what your heart was telling you to do. No matter how wrong it may have seemed to someone outside of your soul, you will always remember your truth inside.

Next time you are faced with a similar situation, choose you. Deal with the fallout of unpleased people right away. And begin to almost immediately start to enjoy the path you know is yours. Do what is in your heart. It is always an opportunity to choose the authentic choices right for you that land us exactly where we are meant to be.

When was the last time you went on an adventure?

Adventure, go on an adventure! Create curiosity about places you've never been before.

There is something so primal, so amazing that sparks on the inside when we leave our comfortable elements and explore new places.

Learning about new things or old things, seeing somewhere for the first time and the imprint that creates in our hearts and souls. A part of you comes out of its shell as you explore new places.

It awakens us. Inspires us. Reminds us of dreams and goals we have yet to desire. It also reminds us of the accomplishment it is to be able to go away and have an adventure.

When you are there and have arrived remember that this is proof of your thoughts becoming reality. You had the idea, created the thoughts, put action behind it and now you are there. Be present and enjoy the moment.

How do you know if it's the right time to take a chance?

Once I have enough ...., I will ....

How often is this said in your life? Usually, it's about money. Once I have enough money, I will buy the car, the house, get a new job, have kids, take that trip, finally leave a bad relation-ship, etc. So, what if you already did have enough, what if you do have what you need to work things out.

Sometimes you are so close that you really need to just go for it. Don't be afraid of getting what you have wanted and worked so hard for, just take it. Know that the money or whatever excuse was in the way will work itself out. Have faith. Put this thought into action.

There are moments that the timing is right, it's the opportunity showing itself and it may never return again. This is your moment. Circumstances may never be this favorable again to do it.

If you find yourself waiting for the enough, here's the news flash- it will never be enough, you will never have exactly enough, and then you will miss your moment. You will never have what it is you wanted because didn't have enough for it.

Take some healthy risks. Have faith and confidence in your decisions. Things might not be perfect, but they may be perfect enough for the right timing. And maybe that was all it was about in the end, timing!

Why not take action today and do something you keep thinking about doing?

Don't just imagine today something you've really wanted to do, pick up the phone and make the call! Look up the details, do the research. Today, take some action instead of just thinking and talking about it. Put some movement behind the thought, get it into motion. Back up your idea and go for it.

Taking chances, doing new things, all create confidence. You have nothing to lose but time. And we all know that we don't control how much time we get to have.

Get moving on your ideas that have maybe so far just been thoughts. Turn them into reality! It's not that hard to do, it's just a shift in your schedule for maybe a few minutes and you never know where that might lead you.

Your Thoughts ... ♡

TWO

Polish Yourself: Getting the Shine Back in Your Life

LET'S TALK ABOUT TAKING PERSONAL
RESPONSIBILITY

Where do you begin?

I have so far to go, you might think and tell yourself. This might be true. Usually at the beginning of starting something new, things tend to hit stagnant spots. Maybe expecting results quicker than rationally possible. Instant results. The moments when things aren't perhaps moving fast enough in the direction we want, the direction we have been working hard on. We do live in a society that seems to have the capability of responding and streaming information quicker and quicker everyday. So, when things aren't so instant and take time to come to fruition, it is easy at those times to get discouraged, feeling like the effort isn't paying off yet, the way you thought it would. Here's the thing- look at how far you have already come. You may not be at the place you want to be at yet, but things are in motion. Where your energy flows things are going to grow.

Do you realize in hindsight the many, many steps you have already taken on your path? The decisions you have already made that made all the dots connect. Maybe right now you feel like your dots are finally connecting or maybe you feel far away from it. Either way you can think back and remember a time before when you felt them all connecting.

Just know, there is always a process. We must experience the many steps in the process to make any vision become reality. And all of a sudden, there we are, fulfilling and living what once seemed so far away.

Where do you belong?

A sense of belonging: we all search for this. It's the feeling of belonging to anything whether it's a club, a church, a team, group of friends, peers, a family, etc. When you are a part of a group that bonds together over like mindedness it feels so good. We then feel the effects of "community". And once we are part of a community, we feel a sense of purpose and ease. We have found a part of ourselves where we belong, and that feels wonderful.

It can bring the feelings of security that we are not alone.

What happens, though, if we can't find that place or group or sense of belonging in our lives? We have all been lonely before. We have all felt left out at some point or not welcome. Well, that is when we need to dig deep and figure out what we're missing. What would be fun, or interesting, or exciting? Is there a sport you used to do and miss? A creative outlet you're wanting to try? Sometimes, we just need to create our own community and get on track to finding and believing you will find it. Bring into your life this sense of belonging! And if you are in a place that you have this sense of community around you, enjoy every bit of it.

You're not happy. Whose fault is that?

Do you blame other people for your situations in life? Like you have no accountability for the things you go through?

Your happiness is a direct link to yourself. To your heart, your mind, your soul. You are the sole owner of your own happiness- no one else!

If other people, make you feel unhappy then it's your job to fix that. It's up to you to change that. You are the one who decides what and how much other people can affect you. It is no one else's job to make sure you are happy in your life. It's your job. You need to do what you need to do to find your smile. Then keep taking action in that direction.

We are blessed with the luxury of choice.

Every minute of everyday we make choices. Yes, shit happens. People can be intolerant or rude to you. But you choose what to do next. You choose how to feel. How to look. How to deal.

This is a job only you can do and do what you must do to start living a happier life. There will always be more we could have or want or need. But right now, you have more than enough if you choose to see it this way.

You are reading this....... You are choosing you. Self care. Health. Self love. Implementing and entertaining new ideas.

Close your eyes, take a breath. Say thank you. Thank you for this breath. This life. The lessons. The love. The forgiveness.

The funny times. The warmth. The mind. The health. The ideas. The sunrise. The stars. The moon. Each new morning.

Are you loving your entire self?

Embrace your ugly. Hug your inner monsters just as much as you hug those glorious, beautiful parts of yourself.

Instead of trying to deny or push or hide away the parts of ourselves that we don't like or find less than desirable, try instead to give them love. It is in this act of loving every bit of ourselves that we find freedom and true happiness within.

I'm not saying that in accepting our flaws that we still shouldn't work on bettering them and ourselves. I am saying that by acknowledging and accepting awareness of our less than desirable parts, we begin to evolve into our truest being through this kind energy.

We know how those moments feel when all is right in our world. Your soul is fed, full, perfect. Maybe it isn't felt often, but isn't that the point? The point is in life we need to feel soul full as much as possible. And it starts with being okay with all of yourself.

We always have bits and pieces that need tweaking, and that is part of our commitment to the journey. And the first step to loving every corner of yourself is exactly that: knowing what hides in those corners and shinning that beautiful soul light on it.

Did you know that you don't need money to be classy?

My grandma used to always tell me, "You don't need money to be classy. Class doesn't cost a thing. And just because someone might have money, it doesn't make them classy."

What a woman!

Have you ever met someone monetarily wealthy that had no class? Maybe you know someone very well like that.

Classy, is classy. No matter who you are, think you are, have achieved or have been given, treating people well is easy and free. It's our nature to be kind.

Kindness, looking someone in the eye, shaking hands when you greet someone, acting and feeling pleased to be in their presence when you meet someone. Walking with you head up, sitting straight. Mind your manners. And don't forget, it's actually easy to be classy and doesn't cost a penny!

And my grandma used to always tell me, too, to get off the phone in thunderstorms and to NEVER take a bath if there's lightening outside!

Do you have healthy boundaries in your relationships?

Creating, making, and enforcing boundaries in relationships isn't always an easy thing to do. It is, however, necessary and one of the most important parts to being in a healthy relationship.

There are times that we don't realize that we need to have certain boundaries until we get pushed into an uncomfortable position or into a corner we don't like.

Have you lost yourself because of the way another person treats you?

If you have ever found yourself involved in a one-sided relationship, you know it is not fun. It sucks to be honest.

So, what keeps us there if ever we are? Sometimes maybe it is with another family member and well, that just always seems to complicate things once we involve family. Why then do we continue to try so hard, give of ourselves when the other person is not invested in the relationship at all. Family or not.

What we can do though is begin to recognize our behavior, their behavior and see how you are handling this on your end. You actually can leave the behavior that locks you into this unhealthy cycle even if you can't leave the relationship itself. Leave the part of the relationship that makes you keep giving and giving without any return from the other person. Change the dynamics on your end. It doesn't have to be announced, or angry. It just has to be authentic.

Again, to set some boundaries for yourself of what you are willing to give and do for someone who doesn't give or do back for you. You can still love someone and not be a victim of them. Honour yourself. Do what is best for you, and the rest will take care of itself. It might get awkward for a minute once you have set your boundaries; but stick to them! It is honestly just a silent shift in your perspective that only you have to know about, that will change how you feel about things. Try to see things differently somehow and disconnect from any hurt that you may take on or feel that perhaps isn't necessary. You will be glad in the long run that you did. And if you need more support, try talking to someone you trust for relationship advice. Walk away if it's time to and do what you feel is right for you. Just decide to make a change with yourself and decide to get rid of the drama too. Life will become much simpler and less stressful.

At any time, your spirit feels like it's being compromised, or mistreated, or forced into being something or someone you are not; then it's time for correction. Time to be aware and immediately begin to take the necessary steps to prevent the hurts from happening again.

The people who value you and respect you will do nothing but support you and your boundaries. With love.

Your own self knowledge and self worth, how you value yourself all matter more than anything in these moments. And how you view yourself tends to project onto others and how they wind up seeing you. Never compromise when it comes to your self worth and your own value. You deserve respect and love so make sure you create the kind of healthy relationships that you deserve and desire.

Do you genuinely have to feel happy to act happy?

What came first, something made you feel happy, so you are now happy? Or, you felt happy and happy things happened? Happiness is a habit, a skill in a sense. Think about What do you bring to the table? I'm not talking about the kitchen table. I am talking about the table of life.

What do you bring emotionally? Are you an easy spirit to be with that feels light? Or is your heart always heavy and full of sorrow? How do you think others would describe you, being in your presence?

I've known people that don't even have the capacity to simply smile at the people that they know around them; never mind being polite to strangers. This is when we must find compassion for others. They don't realize how their behavior can affect others, but we can see visual inner turmoil. Some people show it all on the outside.

On the other hand, I've met people who seem to radiate sunbeams out of their pores! Always happy to see you, be with you, support in any way. The joy they exude is contagious. They may have things happening inside their world that are tough, but you would never know it, they are resilient.

Really think about it, the words you choose, your body language, the choice of conversations you bring up and contribute to. Your comments that you make and how you say them. How you deliver what you have to offer. How you greet others, how you leave people. Consider all of it. Now try to be even more of who you are and want to be. What do you want to bring to the table? The truth is that we have all been both light and dark, upbeat and down, at some point in life. How often you choose to be happy or sad is the thought here. But I do know this much, the more we practice feeling happy, the more happiness we will feel and bring to others. Happiness will only attract more happiness!

How come some people are so lucky?

So, what is the deal with the people that seem to have it all? The abundance makers. Are you one of them? Or do you wish you were one of them? The doers. The ones who are experiencing all of life's funniest, greatest adventures. The people with all the great stories all the time and memories. They have awesome times and travels, having all the best moments surrounded by the best of friends, that you wish you could have.

If you are a spectator in this world and find yourself just watching other people experiencing all the fun, ask yourself why? Why aren't you out there making things happen like the abundant folks are? Really think about that answer. Now cross out 99 percent of the excused you just told yourself.

The only difference between you and them is attitude and perspective. That is all. The way they think and see things. Attitude towards money, free time, knowledge, towards everything. You have to see the positives and be thankful, work towards things, and put yourself out there. But it all begins and ends with how you view your world. Maybe you actually are one of these abundant types and never appreciated it, so never realized just how lucky you really are.

Is your life going the way you want it to?

The way your life is going is a direct reflection of how you view the world around you. Perspective is everything. How you see things dictates what you perceive to be happening.

Have you ever wondered how for some people life is so often wonderful and others it's always negative? To answer that question is to look at how the attitude with the world around them is. Optimistic or pessimistic?

Of course, there are always many different ways to see a situation but try to see the positives even in the negatives. Open up your mind and allow for thinking outside the box. You can handle a lot more than you realize and you can get through anything.

Take the tougher moments as challenges. See all the blessings that maybe you've been missing or taking for granted.

Remember your strengths. Remember things from your past that you have already overcome. View life the best way you can and keep it going. The better your view, the better the life you will have. Perseverance and resilience create strength and the empowerment that you need to do anything you want to. Believe in yourself, believe in your dreams. Conquer your universe.

Attitude. Perspective.

Who do you allow to give you advice?

Take note of who you are taking advice from. If you do take anyone's advice. Not everyone is qualified to tell you what you should do. In fact, there should only be a very well thought out and select sources that you absolutely trust that make the grade to qualify. Depending on the advice I am seeking will then affect the people whom I trust in that particular department of life.

Same goes for when you give and offer advice. Be very thoughtful before you speak. A great rule to go by is only offer advice if someone has actually asked you for it. And remember to be mindful of how you say what you have to say.

Are you taking advantage of being able to be physically active?

Taking care of your body is just as important as taking care of your mind, heart and soul.

If you aren't a fan of movement then it's time to start getting your blood flowing. Your muscles and bones need oxygen just as much as your mind.

Go for a walk, stretch. It doesn't have to cost you a gym membership to get you moving. Instead of watching the clock to see how much longer until it's over, try enjoying that time and space and attention you are giving to your physical self.

Our physical health has a direct impact on our emotional health. Just as much as our emotional health affects our physical health. We are machines inside and when all the parts are working well and together, we are at our best.

The fact that you are able to move around and get around on your own if you can is an independent luxury.

You have energy enough to get around, your body works and allows movement, your mind is clear and sound, honor this. Be so grateful to be able to do things.

Take advantage of having the freedom of independence and momentum. Take advantage of being able to be active and do even more than you are currently doing. Swim, bike, walk, run, twist, jump, meditate, join a team, create a group.

Just don't waste the opportunity you have to be healthy or healthier. Balance is really the key to a happy, healthy you. Take advantage of your freedom of movement.

Ever have trouble with holding back words in an unpleasant moment?

Bite your tongue. Sometimes being quiet in the moment could be the best thing you do. As much as you might want to scream out or be a smart ass and be heard stop yourself. Or before you do speak, think about what it will actually accomplish.

Believe it or not, sometimes the situation will go organically in the direction you hoped for without your interference. Maybe some moments it's better to let other people be the voice.

Not you.

Allow someone else to say what may need to be said. Stepping back and watching the show in certain situations might be the best course of action for you.

You might have things to say, or want to say, but you actually don't always have to say them out loud. You don't have to have the last word. Sometimes just let things happen without your two cents; it might surprise you how the situation unfolds.

What do you do when you have hurt someone?

You've gone too far. You said too much. You have crossed the line and overstepped the boundaries.

We have all had moments like this. Do you then walk away and ignore that you did this? Do you leave it alone for a while and come back to address what happened? Or walk away forever because it is too much to deal with or face because of your own ego?

I guess depending on the situation and who it involves will answer that. Whether you are feeling bad about what happened, or you feel you were justified in your actions, either way you will eventually need to address this, if even just for yourself to confront what you did. Talk about it, walk through it once again and work on it, if it's someone that you care about how they feel.

People usually don't set out intentionally to hurt others. In fact, our true nature is actually kindness for the majority of us. It may not seem that way all the time but it's true. But in those times where we have gone too far, caused another pain with our actions or words then we do need to communicate our sincere remorse for what we caused. Let them know we care and feel concern despite what it may seem.

It's tough to own our shit sometimes when we get messy. But it's part of the journey. Use it to grow, use it to do and be better. After all, we are only human, and we are very good at making mistakes. But we can also learn to be very good at fixing things too.

Why should we apologize?

The art of an apology. What does that even mean? What is an apology anyway? And why is it so darn important?

Because it is the validation that we have been heard. The validation that there is recognition to the hurt or wrongdoing done to us.

For when we apologize to others and say sorry, we are acknowledging we were in the wrong, whether that was our intent or not. But it is just as important to the apologizer as it is to the victim. Hopefully, it soothes the pain of knowing you caused pain to someone, while trying to take away some of the pain you may have caused them.

Now, how often do you apologize to yourself? This is very important! Sometimes we allow others to walk on us. Maybe we put ourselves in positions that may cause ourselves harm or hurt. Maybe we haven't been talking very nicely or treating ourselves with the respect we deserve. As important as it is to hear someone say, "I'm sorry", it is equally, if not more important, to say it to yourself.

Now that you have done that move forward. Forgive. If you never get the apology from another person that you should have, keep on moving. Sometimes, the best apologies you accept you may have never heard. Don't let it or them take away from who you are. You know what is proper, and let it go. Apologies are one of the strongest acts we control and can do; it is the opposite of being weak to admit you're wrong. It actually takes courage and vulnerability to tell someone you are sorry. That equals strength.

HO'OPONOPONO
(Hawaiian Prayer)

I love you.
I am sorry.
Forgive me.
Thank you.

Repeat! Over and over again.

"HO'OPONOPONO is a process by which we can forgive others to whom we are connected. Practicing Ho'oponopono allows you to cut the Aka connection in a very positive loving way. Knowing that you can make the connection brand new. When you become right with others, you become right with yourself." - *Psychology Today*

HO'OPONOPONO is an ancient Hawaiian practice still in use today, well known for the miracle it does in clearing negativity from one's mind and thought.

Did you know that everything is temporary, especially our feelings?

We are always in perpetual motion. Everything is changing at all times around us. Look at the seasons of the year, for example. Every day, every minute there are things in motion. And our emotions are always evolving too. Just because we are going through something doesn't mean we will forever be stuck in that something. Yes, some situations will take a lifetime to deal with but remember how you feel right now doesn't mean you have to feel that way forever.

There was a time in my life that was so unbearable it took every ounce of what little strength I felt I had left to not end it myself. I would tell myself that if I just made it through another minute, I can surely make it through one more. In the moment I couldn't even imagine feeling so awful, so broken, for another day. But I didn't have to think so far ahead, just for the moment and then that turned into another day, and another day. But the one thing inside of me that kept screaming was that things had to get better with time. Maybe not right away, but eventually my life would look different. One day my life would be one that I choose. One day I would live in peace and happiness because I wanted that so much. Life takes turns that we don't expect or see coming sometimes. Things we don't choose happen to us. And it may be that you can't imagine how you will move forward, you don't have a clue how to handle your emotions that run your every breath, take over every cell and thought. But it is temporary. Whether you get over what has happened, or you find a new normal that involves accepting your feelings, or some way to make peace with it, things will get better. As humans we are constantly evolving, growing, getting older, changing. Just know, how we are and how we feel can evolve and will evolve in time. One day you can think about how something made you grow and wonder how you can somehow benefit from it.

Remember everything is temporary. There are necessary reasons for slow down cycles. It gives us time to clean out, sort out, shout out, and acknowledge shit we have going on. We are definitely in the moment when we have these days, so be in it. It's not forever.

And reach out, people love to be chosen to be confided in. If you find yourself in this place more often than any other space, find a professional or group that can help guide you or give you the tools you may need to feel better.

When was the last time you gave yourself a hug?

The smarter you tell yourself you are- the smarter you will be. It's a fact.

If your internal voice starts to speak to yourself in positive ways, you will actually begin to notice that these things are all true.

Be as kind to yourself as you would be to a new friend. When we meet someone for the first time, we notice all kinds of things about them. When we meet someone that we really enjoy their company we think about how wonderful they are, and all the lovely traits that make them so loveable.

Try meeting yourself again or maybe for the first time. Give yourself internal pats on the back for all the little things that make you tick. All the neat stuff you forgot about yourself, smile and notice again. And thank yourself for being smart.

You can notice all the beauty that surrounds you and that is because you have attracted it to you like a magnet. Like attracts like. So, as you see, you are, and will be.

Your Thoughts ... ♡

THREE

Don't Let the Shine Fade: Dealing with Setbacks

DEALING WITH FEAR, JUDGEMENT, SELF-DOUBT, OR GRIEF/LOSS

When life gets messy, what can you do?

Do you ever have that internal drag of your emotions, just feeling off perhaps, even messy? Maybe you're in a situation in life that you can't fix in a day, and just thinking about it isn't enough to make it go away. There will always be times when life gets a little messy or a lot messy. Usually, messy clean-ups are a process, just like spilt milk. It happens, you see it happen, you realize what has happened, you gather the tools you need for the job, and you get it done. It is always one step at a time. Emotional messes need and deserve time to clean up. Another way to see it is transition- the changes will occur and may be uncomfortable, but it will be worth the work and effort in the end. It could even be someone else that has made the mess and you are left to clean it up. Just remember there is always something to learn or grow or take away from these moments.

How can we be kinder?

Everyone of us has opinions, thoughts, and judgments at times. Sometimes more than other times, people can be very judgemental, and yet there are those who don't seem to be very much at all. We can find solace in friendships and relationships where we feel free of judgement. We feel these are more of an unconditional love compared to being around people who are constantly criticizing, or act dissatisfied with who you are. Maybe there's times we do need a kick in the ass, but that should be out of love and guidance. When we feel judged, it is not out of a space of love but maybe out of ignorance or maybe jealousy.

How often do you find yourself judging others? How do you judge yourself? What do you do in situations when you know people have judged you? Try for a start just one day of quieting the voices in your head that are judging yourself and others. Whenever you feel the impulse to make a negative judgment replace it quickly with a compliment. Keep on doing this and eventually your mind will be a much happier place! Whether we acknowledge it or not- we are never at our best when bringing down others even if it's only in our head.

Is it worth the fight?

Pick your battles. There are times in our lives that conflict is more prominent than other times. People in relationships fight, and any relationship we engage in that is important, will sooner or later bring conflict. Parents, children, friends, family, coworkers, bosses... conflict with them is sometimes inevitable. In any and every deep relationship that you open yourself up to and allow feelings, vulnerability and growth, there will almost guaranteed be an issue at some point or disagreement.

When should we let something go through and slip by? When do we instead choose battle or confrontation?

When we choose to confront someone with our feelings, we run the risk of further damage to the relationship and or situation. But we have now also shifted the energy that must create change, for better or worse. The fact is that relationships require honesty. Each person must share their truth so that their feelings for one another grow and develop. And there are many times things can be dropped or let go (if it's not harming you internally for not speaking up).

We only control ourselves. In the process of confronting someone, you must be prepared for it to go in a completely different direction than the one you intended.

In a perfect world, our feelings would be validated as soon as we communicated them. People would instantly get what we're trying to say. But that is quite rare. Usually, it will take a little massaging and word fumbling to get the point across properly, because we are all different in the way we perceive things. Just think about how much pain and suffering is caused solely by miscommunication.

We become so vulnerable when we open up and share our feelings with someone. This takes great courage and strength. Going in with good intentions of working something out as to better the relationship that you care so much about is also to be brave, and so necessary to try to communicate with the hopes of resolving the conflict.

Ask yourself if this will matter still next week? Next month will this issue still be top of mind? How about in a year will this still be important, and still, you are remembering the problem? Or will it simply vanish and become a memory or maybe entirely forgotten? Maybe there are bigger fish to fry or maybe this is the big fish that needs to get fried.

Do you sometimes overreact?

Don't make it bigger than it is. You don't have to take something minor or small and blow it up to be a huge deal.

Do you try and force situations?

"Loose plans create loose responses!" I have to laugh as I write this.... A friend and I were playing tennis and the fellows on the adjoining court were talking about a date that went sideways. And that was the quote I took from their hilarious conversation. I think we have all been witness on either side of that saying at some point in our lives!

Maybe deep inside we really didn't want to be with the other person, or on the flip side kept trying with someone that had no interest to be with us.

Either way, it reminds us to never try and force situations. If you want to set up something with someone, try to. If not don't. Just trust that things will organically work out as they should and how they should. In the end you always know that someone out there has your back!! Trust it! There could be reasons that thing didn't come together in the first place that you may never know of, and that could be a blessing in disguise.

♡

Do you keep beating a dead horse?

Beating a dead horse. I get it—we all need to vent about what is bothering us sometimes. But there's that and then there is never moving past it. Are you constantly complaining about the same things over and over? Is your story on repeat whenever you have an audience that is willing to listen to you?

It is probably in your best interest to stop doing that if you are doing that. Not only does it get extremely annoying to listen to again and again, but it is actually making you worse instead of better.

The process of venting is just that: letting something out that is about to make you blow up or explode.

When you constantly repeat the same complaint, it will only bring you down. It will keep you upset. It will keep you feeling negative, and you really won't and don't feel good about yourself in this moment. It is not our highest form when we keep replaying a negative situation over and over again without making any positive changes to it.

I'm talking about that habitual complainer that is always stuck in a funk. It seems there are never solutions only ever-growing problems.

It's easy to try to offer a positive spin on their situations, or a twist on their perspective. Maybe offering up solutions to help their problems.

What is actually happening when we do that is we are giving and transferring our energy to them. We are then feeding the emotional vampires. And, believe me, they never get full.

This will leave you emotionally drained and exhausted. And engaging in this twisted dance over and over only encourages more of this toxic behavior pattern.

It's not up to you to change people and you are never obligated to have to help others with their emotional habits. You can be a great listener and friend and leave it at that. You never have to give away your energy to an endless pit. The endless pit that prefers it that way. Silently set your boundaries, make the choice to not give into this anymore and see what a difference it will make.

If you struggle with blaming your failures on other people, know that it will never make you successful. It is the opposite. You must look at yourself. Look hard at your own part of your failure. I know it's an inside job.

You can only point your fingers at others for so long until you realize that you are you own problem. It's not easy to admit it's your own shit that you need to own.

But guess what? It's also not the end of the world. It is success. The universe will not shut down because you came clean with yourself. It will though open up. It will create more opportunities to fix what needs to be in order to get you to where your soul can work at it's highest and best use.

This is exactly where you need to be to win. To succeed in life. This is the real success, not failure! Begin to look at your perspective, sort out where you need to let this go to, and let it go. Move on! And for goodness' sake stop annoying people with the same old situation. It is also a great idea to throw away any negative texts or letters or emails. Only keep the positive notes, get rid of the nasty ones they serve you no purpose other than to remind you of hurt. The happy ones can remind you of the better moments. Read these often and make yourself smile.

Do you allow yourself to get too involved in other people's problems?

Getting pulled into battles that are not your own can happen easily, and it can happen often. And maybe you never even realized that it wasn't your fight to begin with. I know that it happens in our daily life; the opportunity to allow someone else's mood or energy positive and negative into our own psyche.

When other people have a problem or recurring problem that never seems to have resolution or resolve and keep you informed and involved in it- well, you are now a piece of this battle. It could be a fight someone you care about is having and you want to help, want to be there for them, help fix it. We tend to want to be a part of solutions sometimes and then by default we involve ourselves. We involve ourselves in places and in scenarios where we don't belong. Where we actually have no business being.

Are you guilty of taking on other people's shit?

You might think that it shows your commitment as a good friend or partner, but it's actually not your problem.

Taking on issues that belong to other people will only drain you of your life force and prevent you from focusing on your own stuff.

We've all got stuff that can use our own attention. And sometimes it may seem easier to deal and focus on other people's stuff instead of facing our own.

Put that energy into you. Being there for someone also has its healthy boundaries. Know where your boundaries are and take care of your stuff first.

It is easy and human to feel emotional for people we love and care about. But when this shifts into becoming a detriment to your own life, your own moods and livelihood, then you need to back away. Back off their life and focus again on your own. Mind your own business. Trust that they will figure out themselves, after all it's not about you anyway! It's one thing to listen and it's entirely another to have their situation turn into your problem. Simplify your life as much as you can.

Do you struggle with saying "NO"?

Believe it, saying "no" can be one of the hardest things in the world sometimes to do. Two simple letters with an outstanding result. We've all been there. We've all been worried to let others down when asked to do something or to give something. I used to struggle at the grocery store till to say "no" to donate a dollar to a charity every time I shopped, even though I donate much money every year to charity and my time volunteering. I had to justify heavily to myself first to eventually feel okay saying no thanks not today. Crazy.

There is definitely an art to saying "no" to offers that we truly don't want to take. And there is a freedom that comes with us being honest in the beginning when given the almighty chance.

We've all been pushed before by someone, a salesperson, friend, family member, any one out in the community can try to get something out of you or from you. But knowing you have the backbone and strength to stand up for yourself is golden. And you will feel so much better getting rid of this idea or favor or whatever purchase you really didn't want or need right from the start.

Here are a couple suggestions for you should you find yourself struggling with saying no to people.

1. Thank them for the opportunity and SAY "NO".
2. If it's an invitation and it does matter to you because it involves someone you care about, but you just don't feel like you can do it right then, suggest another time or date you could make it work. This way they know you care. If it isn't someone in your inner circle just refer to #1.

I know there is an infinite number of different requests and needs out there. But you have to do what is right for you. Don't worry about letting someone down if it doesn't seem right for you. They will get over it. However, it will be a lot more to get over if you hold resentment for doing something you didn't authentically wish to do from the start. Saying "no" to things or people is a personal decision for you, not them. And just the same on the flip side, try not to take a NO from someone else personally.

We all know the consequence it takes on us when we find ourselves not happy to be doing things, we never wanted to do in the first place. So, save yourself the grief up front. The more you practise this, the easier it gets. Take time if you need to think about your answer first before you respond, that should be respected no matter what. And too should your decision in the end.

How do you deal with frustrating people in your life that won't change?

First off, is it out of line to want or ask someone to change? Is it fair that we request something different from someone we love? Absolutely, yes, it is okay. This is growth in a relationship or should be looked at that way. If someone you care about, you are in a relationship with that matters to you is doing something that keeps challenging you or your morals, you always have the option of communication. Communicate in a loving way that lets this person know what is going on with you. This then gives them the opportunity to change as you asked or not. You can always look back and remember you tried. Needing something from someone that they aren't giving to you might be as simple as the fact that they didn't even know you needed that. So always try talking about things first.

When someone is bothering you, pushing you or getting under your skin, there's only one thing you can do. Change yourself. Your thought patterns on the subject, your energy you normally feel towards it; do something different. Try reacting in a new way. Maybe just ignore them or laugh it off. Einstein said, "The definition of insanity is doing the same thing over and over and expecting a different result."

Think about that.

Stop putting so much energy into relationships and people that aren't good for you. If they're not good to you, then they are not good for you. Maybe not forever, but for right now.

There are times we fight to get people who don't value us as we should be valued to see us the way we want them to; but why should you have to try to convince someone to see your beauty if it's not obvious to them? Or constantly battle over respecting your boundaries in the relationship?

Put all that effort you spend trying to convince someone of your worth into someone who sees all you are worth. Put the ones who get you and appreciate your unique self to the very top of your totem pole.

If someone can't see the true spirit of your beautiful self, then you need to realize it is to their disadvantage not yours. Let it be. Forgive them. Forget them. Change your focus and attention on the real souls that not only get you but love you. Make these people your priority and make sure you tell them how important they are to you too.

Are you being too hard on yourself?

Some days emotions can overrun you. They can run all that is happening, and it may feel like every response you have is emotional. Maybe someone triggered you. Maybe it's a situation that has you feeling like this, none the less it happens.

Don't feel bad about it, though. A good cry, a good freak out, it's all part of life. Obviously, if you are experiencing a day like that it has probably been building up for some time. It doesn't make you negative or a bad person when you have these moments, it makes you simply human.

Let it ride. Feel what you feel. Get a good sleep and wake up new. You are so lovable; it isn't even funny!

Is it time to step back?

Sometimes you just need to back off. When you find yourself in a situation where you know it isn't working, or like you have lost control over it we tend to do the opposite and struggle to hold onto it.

The more we try to force ourselves or our beliefs on a situation that isn't in our favour the further away from us it will seem to get. Something inside us may be screaming don't give up, not yet, you haven't won. But the best idea would be to take a walk. It doesn't mean you gave up or it's even over, but you need a repositioning.

This will stick with you of course but ease up. Regain your power. Regain your composure and back off for a bit. Then see what organically happens without being forced to happen, and you may not like it but that's okay. You will survive.

Are you having a day you need to wash off?

Some days are just tougher than others. You might feel like you have been hit by a Mac truck as you watch the rapid rate of deconstruction happening around you. You may be left wondering how things fell apart so fast.

It's hard not to fall completely into a downward spiral once things begin to crumble. The truth is some days are just going to be like that. Life isn't always pretty, so these are the challenges that create the perfect crappy storm.

Think about it, a storm requires many factors to turn into a super-cell and then even more to spawn itself into a tornado. Pretty much exactly like a shitty day can take off.

Best news ever: you get another chance to reset and start over tomorrow. Or maybe later, or tonight. We always can restart. Sleep it off, wash it off in the shower, crank some loud awesome music, just start new. It is really just the decision you make to wash it off. That is the greatest part, the ability to reset and start again.

Sometimes when we don't feel like we are connecting with anyone, just connect with yourself. Put on the music that moves you, the lyrics that make you feel. Watch a movie that inspires you or get into a really good book that transforms your world or makes you feel understood. The arts are such a gift and a wonderful way to help our souls in times when we do really feel alone.

This doesn't mean that everything that went wrong disappears. But maybe it can give time to settle down a bit. Time can give new perspective and rest thinking so much about it.

Did you stop and think there might be more to someone's behavior than what seems obvious?

You never really know what is going on inside of people. We might be running about our days and so easily judge others' behavior or actions and reactions, without any thoughts that there could be more to it.

Not everyone wears their feelings on their sleeves, and some people wear too much of their emotions where everyone can see.

If we take the time before we address something or give people the chance to speak, maybe we will hear something we didn't hear before. Giving them the benefit of doubt, not ignoring the possibility that there may be something else going on that you don't see.

You just never know what someone might be going through. So be kind out there. Smile as much as you can; smiling is contagious. It's a good thing! Try to feel happy when you see others are feeling happy around you. Be a good human. After all, it actually takes way less energy to be happy than upset. So, before anyone overreacts or takes something personal that isn't meant to be, think about other possibilities like there might just be something else going on with someone.

Do you ever stand up for other people?

Having an advocate in your corner is a luxury and a luxury you should never take for granted.

When there is someone that believes in you, and gets you, and understands your situation that is what I call a blessing. So often people don't have a voice of their own that they can use in certain situations, and that is where someone else's voice is so important. Someone else that can speak up for them.

When that happens and someone speaks up for you, something wonderful begins to shift in the situation. The narrative begins to change. You begin to feel validated. When we feel validated, we feel understood and connected.

Everyone needs to have someone in their corner. And for many of us that isn't always the case. That is why I call it a luxury. It makes us feel good to know someone has our back. So, whether you have an advocate in your life often, or sometimes have one, appreciate it. Appreciate them. There are always times when things are dependant too on the situation; think about this: for whom or when have you ever been an advocate for someone else? Everybody needs that sometimes.

How do you handle yourself when someone has hurt you?

When people hurt other people whether intentionally or not, they are hurting themselves even more.

So often when we get hurt by someone, we instantly go into a defensive mode. We start by judging them. This reaction is totally natural, especially when we have been hurt.

What if instead of reacting badly and staying hurt, we realize how much this person who did this to you must be hurting inside. Hurting so badly that they can't help what they are doing to others, or maybe don't even realize what they are doing.

Having compassion for another person's pain who has hurt you will ultimately free you from the hurt caused by them.

Step back, take a breath. Forgive. When you choose to forgive others, it is ultimately about freeing yourself from the negative emotions that unresolved issues harbor. You aren't forgiving someone for them, you are forgiving someone for yourself. It really is as easy as telling yourself that you choose to forgive them. You may experience other emotions, but you will begin to shift and move on with the idea of letting go of unwanted bitterness. And feel better. Choose to let it pass. Just because you chose to move on doesn't mean you have to forget about it, it just says that you have better things to focus on in your life. This is also relevant to how badly you feel and the depth of hurt you were caused to feel. I get it: not all situations are created equally. In this example it may apply to the less major situations. Ones that won't change your life or alter your world forever or very long.

If you are interested in talking to the person that hurt you about their behaviour, and how it affected you here's a good way to go about it.

Before we speak especially when emotions are involved ask yourself to THINK.

THINK

T: TRUTHFUL

H: HONEST

I: IS IT HURTFUL

N: NECESSARY

K: KIND

Once you have gone through all these questions, feel confident in your words. Remember your self worth. You deserve to be respected. You can then take what you have learned from the situation and use it to better yourself.

How can you help heal from losing someone?

When you lose someone important in your life, they are irreplaceable. There will never be another one of them. You must get used to their special energy and love being gone.

You never get over it. You just get used to missing them. It becomes normal eventually and will forever remain a part of your psyche.

You can celebrate these beautiful souls in so many wonderful ways. Something that I found works for me is to surround myself with people that possess the similar traits as the ones I am missing. It could be a great sense of humor, or silliness, anything that you miss. Notice what you miss so much and try to find it around you in other ways.

Even though you can't bring them back, and even with finding pieces of them in others will never replace them; it can bring you a bit of comfort and maybe a smile in that moment.

Have you done any mental house keeping lately?

There are always moments we have had that are less than favourable. Memories, situations that maybe we didn't deal with in the moment. We put it away on a back shelf of our mind and perhaps in the moment took the high road or a different road than the road that led to closure.

Rest assured those ugly, uncomfortable moments will probably reappear and resurface. And once again, no matter what triggered it, you are presented again with that yuck moment from a time gone by.

It is very important to process that thought. Accept that pain, hurt, done-wrong. It doesn't mean you accept being treated wrong, it did happen so now look it over and choose forgiveness. Whether you feel it or not, do it for you.

Most times the perpetrator doesn't even know what they did. They have no clue the impact their choice of words or decisions of ill will towards you hurt so much. And they honestly don't need to know, because chances are, they still won't get it. Or maybe it's a situation you brought on yourself and it's just time to let it go for good.

As much as you dread cleaning out the back of your closets or drawers, the time eventually comes when you have to. You might not like it, but once it's cleaned out, you feel so good. Our minds need tidying and organizing too. Clean up, clean out, get rid of the crap taking up precious real estate up there and make space for new happiness.

It is just like when you have been avoiding dealing with something.

When we put off dealing with something it will always come back around again until we fix it and face it.

Sometimes things may be too heavy in the moment, and you need more time to process and to properly place it. It will resurface and present to you again another opportunity to deal with it and move on.

Look at it this way: your air conditioner breaks down at the end of summer. You can wait to fix it as the colder months are ahead. Maybe next spring or summer, you can do it then because right now it isn't needed and doesn't matter. But you will have to eventually fix it if you want to be comfortable.

So, here's the takeaway from this: clean out your mental closets and drawers and darn it fix your air conditioner!

Cracking under pressure or are you upping your game under pressure?

When we come under strain and hit the breaking point it forces us to act.

Reacting is cracking because it actually means we've lost control and involves an involuntary response. Which usually then we can add an extra step afterwards that will include clean up.

Instead, if we step up our game under pressure or teach ourselves to slow the reaction time down enough that it no longer is a reaction it becomes an action, and action is a choice. Choice is now a decision that you thought through and decided on. This doesn't eliminate automatically regret or disappointment, but you did go into it with more consciousness.

Acknowledgment in the moment is key. Sometimes we are pushed or triggered resulting from past experiences, but knowing that, is the beginning of better decision making.

We can start to design more and more aspects of our future by practising our responses to everyday situations. Then the big stuff when it shows up won't be so scary, leading us to calmly choose what we want.

Your Thoughts ... ♡

FOUR

Blazing Brilliance: Embrace Gratitude

HOW BEING GRATEFUL CAN HELP YOU STAY ON THE
RIGHT PATH

Do you realize how lucky you are?

If every morning when you wake up and life is just as it was when you fell asleep, be happy. Even if it's not where you want to be or whether you are in a good place, or needing change, just be grateful.

Life can change in seconds with things that we can not control. It's time to wake up and realize how lucky you already are! How blessed you already are! How anything is in your reach! You can manage and make changes if needed. And when life is easy and automatic whether that seems boring to you or dull- that's the calm. The actual peace of getting to just wake up without pain, fear, mourning, sadness, regret, heart and soul break, any emotions that you didn't choose, like loss.

I know about this. After my mom died, I remember thinking about all the usual days that I took for granted because they seemed the same as always. Mundane and predictable. What I never realized was how luxurious those days actually were. Because after losing my mom, waking up everyday became one of the hardest parts of my life. It wasn't automatic anymore; it was so difficult to imagine and live another day of hell without her. Immense sadness and sorrow occupied my every cell every moment for so long. It took a long time to be okay with our new normal without her. I don't know if it's ever okay, but you have to adapt and accept what you can't change. To this day, I am always grateful to wake up and have my life exactly as it was the night before when I laid my head down, messy or not, emotions or situations that need resolving or not-it's still an amazing day and all parts of my world are intact. Don't take these moments for granted, because life can change so fast.

It's a new day, so cherish it! Be happy it's off to a great, easy start. And even if it's not- make it that way.

Do you realize how much you have to look forward to?

Get excited! The future is still coming!!!

Did you know that with every thought, idea, design that you are actually creating in your mind what is yet to come?

It's true! With positive thinking, you create a vibration and as you send those thoughts and feelings outwards like a boomerang, they will return to you. Think about your best idea of life for yourself, without any boundaries or excuses. If you had all the wishes in the world for yourself, what would you wish for?

All your dreams have the ability to come true. Period. The key to it is to believe and to do the work to follow through with them. It all starts with your creativity and desire of the life you wish for. There are no rules when it comes to this. There are no boundaries on what you can or can't have except for the ones you put on yourself. The only excuses for not attaining what you want is down to the ones you make for yourself. There is no such thing as problems, only solutions!

Try to once a day think about your happiness. What does that include? Be selfish, be honest. Know that you can have anything and everything you can imagine. Feel it now! Picture all the glory and money or love or whatever homes, cars, family, vacations, the lifestyle everything and anything. Now make a dream board outside of your head with all these dreams. It's the practice of visualization.

You can pin pictures or words that inspire you, dollar signs, or symbols of happiness. Put them on a cork board or poster paper. You can curl the pages of magazines that you keep around and flip back to as a reminder to yourself.

The key is to remind yourself as often as you can of your dreams. Remind yourself how it is going to feel and feel it again and again, over and over. Act as if it's here. Look back at all the things you have already brought to your life today. Now look forward and work on the next best things that you want in this life.

Is the sun shining outside your window?

Maybe you have to imagine it just shining inside your mind and heart and soul.

Feel the energy that is being produced and spread by this giant planet of light. Feel physically the warmth as you close your eyes, running from the bottom of your toes, rising up slowly, warming all the way past your knees, thighs, hips, up through your lower back. As its rays are bright and warm also know that this light is healing. Rising up further through your abdomen and belly, begin to breathe it into your lungs and up your chest, to your heart center, your shoulders, elbows, hands and all the way to the top of your neck, ears, and head. Stay here. Breathe. Inhale warmth, love, protected breath inhale light. Exhale and let out the dark, dust and not needed energy. Exhale. Make space for love. Take a few deep breaths and reset yourself for your day or use this technique to reset yourself for the moment you find yourself in. know that the sun is always shining on inside of you.

Are you focusing too much on the wrong things?

We don't take anything with us when we leave here. No money, clothing, cars, gifts, pictures, our home, books, nothing—not even our bodies. Nothing of material value comes with us when we go. Even if you are obsessed with making the outside of yourself look good, you should definitely make sure the inside of you looks even better. The most important things that matter in this world are your relationships. The love. The people, the souls. The ones you choose to spend your time and energy with. The ones you share and make the memories, sacred moments, laughter, tears, magic, the fun, feels, time. That's it. The people we love, loved, and would choose to do it with all over again if we could. When you look at where you put your energy in your life, remember balance is always the best, but remember, too, that it's how our friends, family and soulmates made us love. How we felt we treated them that's most important. If you are constantly focused on the outer parts of your world, maybe realize that the most important parts don't cost a dime and are an inside job. It's wonderful to enjoy 'things' but it's always better when you have someone to share them with.

What do you do as soon as you wake up?

Waking up after sleeping is a very sensitive time. If even for a few minutes sit in silence, eyes open or closed. Think about a goal or goals that you want to accomplish. Reflect on the victories that you have already accomplished. Remember all the wonderful things you are thankful for. Smile. Now imagine the feeling once you have achieved and accomplished the goals you imagine and long for. How does it feel to be thankful for all that you have and have already done in your life? How does it feel? This is a simple way of meditation and manifestation for designing your day ahead. It doesn't have to be complicated. Just simply thoughts and gratitude. Which then brings on more of the same.

There are days that I just want peace. Peace in my heart, my mind, my home, my soul, peace in my family. A day of everyone getting along in my world peacefully. So, I begin my morning with thoughts of peace and good memories of peaceful times. Then there are days that I imagine my future; the imaginary space where I have already manifested and brought to reality all my financial, emotional, relationships, career, and health dreams. Put the first focus and thoughts here first thing in your day, rather than a list of what you are lacking. Try setting up your mind without any outside influences. Set up your mind before you check your phone or devices. Checking your social media accounts or email before taking the time to design your day is not good. When you are already looking at other people's lives before you have taken any time to look at your own is just like walking around aimlessly for the rest of the day. It will do nothing but distract you from what wonderful thoughts you may have missed because you are too busy watching someone else's life, and now are influenced by exterior motives or intentions that are not truly your own. So, think about that if you are someone that instantly picks up your phone as soon as you are conscious. Change that habit. Trust me your life will be so much better. Try thinking about you first.

It's an easy thing to do, and if you do it everyday, it will create a much better experience. And go back to those re-affirming, positive thoughts throughout your day and keep them in mind.

When was the last time you did something unexpected for someone else?

Do something nice for someone else. Not because you were asked to. Not because you feel you have to. Do it because you want to. Giving is a bit of a selfish act in the sense that in the process of it, it makes you feel good too. And there's nothing wrong with that!

The giving of energy, thoughts, time, in anyway without any kind of hidden agenda is awesome.

What we get back is internal, it's the thought of putting a smile on someone's face and warming their heart. We feel good; they feel good. Think of the chain reaction of giving to someone, doing something unexpected and kind; the happiness will spread, creating more of the same. Can you think about times when someone surprised you with a notion of kindness or a gesture of love that you weren't expecting, and for seemingly no reason at all but just because you are special? Remember how that made you feel?

You have this power to make this happen. You have the power to lift up other people. Isn't that amazing!

How can you quickly shift your emotions when you most need to?

Gratitude, period. Or do something nice for someone, period. When life gets heavy, and you feel like your heart just can't take anymore hurt or pain or sadness, you have to try something different. Try in that moment to just pause, take a breath, and slow down. Try to clear or move your thoughts for just a single moment and no matter how much it hurts say thank you. That's all. Thank you.

It sounds crazy but if you can find gratitude in a most difficult moment your feelings begin to shift, and everything will begin to shift too. It doesn't mean you are inviting more pain to yourself by being thankful; it's simply acknowledging you are alive. There is more to you than this moment. You know happiness, you have loved, continue to love, you also have the capacity to mourn a loss and feel hurt because you know love. It really is the hard, tough gift of transformation taking place. Whether welcomed or not. Perhaps it was something brought on by your own choices or maybe it's a situation brought on by the fact that crappy shit sometimes happens. Remember that these are the motions that we sometimes have to go through, but you will get through. Somehow find a way to be thankful and you will start to feel better.

Do something nice for someone else. Yes, give of yourself the exact good vibes you don't think you even possess in that moment.

Send a text to a friend or family member telling them you love them. Put some positivity out there in the airwaves. Write a note and put it on your bathroom mirror telling your family or roommates they are awesome! Compliment a stranger at the grocery store or bank or restaurant. The quicker you shift into an act of kindness the quicker you will shake off the blues. FACT!

Remind yourself that everything is temporary. Time passes, and circumstances are always changing.

But good things, good people, good times, a good view, a good memory, a good laugh, a good joke, a good cry, a good hug, a good smile, anything can be turned around into a good thing.

Bad times lead the way to appreciation and realization of how lucky we are to have good times. Happiness is a choice, and it is created. So, if you aren't seeing much happy lately go out and make some!

Do you ever think about the power you possess when it comes to your feelings?

Wherever you might be today or find yourself right now emotionally, practise the feeling of joy! Fake it, if you have to. Put as much aside as you can if you are in a negative space. Tell yourself, "Today I choose to be joyful, right now I choose to be joyful! Today I will see the happy, joyful things and moments put on my path in front of me."

Other things may try and get in the way, don't let them! Push back and let things slide. Promise yourself this and say, "I am going to smile, and giggle today! I will not let stress get the better of me! Look at how awesome this........................ is! Look at how awesome I am!! Today I will see the moments I may have otherwise missed, the simple, enjoyable moments. Today I want my heart to be light." Pick a song that makes you move and keep it in your head and remind yourself, "today I choose joy, I am joy!!"

At what cost are you holding onto something or someone that you need to let go of?

We are often so afraid of rejection that sometimes staying in a toxic relationship or environment that constantly rejects us becomes less frightening than moving on or moving out.

It could be the idea of the relationship you wished it would be and not giving up on it is all you know, even though you deep down know it won't change. It could be a work environment that is toxic. There are many different places in our lives that we may put up with more negativity than in others. But in all honesty, once you realize you tried your best, put it all in, been honest with yourself, and still the results are the same, then it's probably time to make a new plan. It's different for every scenario, but ultimately done means change. Change, that scary thing lingering on the distant or not so distant horizon.

Don't fear change, friends. Change that we know we need to see, change that we can welcome. The change we choose. Change is so frightening to most people. Some people though actually get off on it and love it; so much so it can become addictive, and they can't sit still.

If you know you are in a bad place and need to change something, but you are scared to do it, think about coming to the end of your journey on earth. Will you be mad at yourself for not taking the risks into the unknown? Or will you be okay with your decision to stay put?

An idea that starts with you beginning to be comfortable with a change. Viewing yourself in a better situation and deserving of a more positive experience. So often we stay in less than desirable spaces because we fear the unknown, and then find ourselves years down the road still stuck in something we don't enjoy. The cost to ourselves for staying stuck can lead to major health problems, drama that is unnecessary. Many undesirable things can and will arise when we refuse to better our lives when we know we need to and should. Ignoring your soul's path and missing out on the experiences waiting for you, mean that you're turning your back on your higher purpose. These are opportunities you are meant to have. A path you were meant to tread. Especially once you have made a decision that you know in your heart is true.

We tend to actually make decisions quickly but seem to stagger when it comes time to follow through, mostly when it means life will look different.

Create a new plan, a new strategy. Space in your life for all the good things you deserve. You deserve the best this life has to offer. Don't ever be afraid to make things better for yourself. Detach yourself from any outcome and see where it takes you. The journey will be worth the fear of the unknown and even if things wind up looking much different than you thought, you at least now trust yourself enough and have a new confidence that tells you things don't have to be so scary out there. Listen to your gut, and do what is right for you.

Things always have a way of working out. It's just about how we choose to see them! Don't be afraid of new opportunities. They might not show up often, but sometimes we are offered an opportunity that we didn't see coming.

This can be overwhelming as much as exciting. Make sure it's something you would like to invest your energy into. And don't be scared to say YES! Go for it. Or feel confident saying no if it's not right for you. You will always learn along the way what you will need to know. You don't have to have the answers up front; the answers will come with the experience.

Never let fear be your guide. Fear is a trap, a trap that we allow ourselves to fall into. It can be debilitating. It's just life, after all. You will always bounce back. For sure differently than when you started as your evolution continues throughout all the lessons and opportunities that present themselves. You will be okay! Enjoy yourself out there and have fun.

Go in with your heart and mind open. Welcome the new, the unexpected. Embrace the challenges. Life would be so boring otherwise.

Have you thought about how special the people you love are?

In memory of.........

It's been so long since I heard your voice tell me you love me. Since I've heard your laugh. Seeing your beautiful smile and face, your smell. It's been so long since I felt your hugs, and your presence around me. It has been so long that I have had to live without you. Without your love. Just talking about everything and nothing. Always knowing you had my back and supported me, helping to guide me through this crazy life. All gone and to never return at least while you're up there and I am here. I would do anything for you to be back. Life really isn't fair sometimes. All I can do now is talk about your beauty, your amazing spirit, and hope to carry on a part of you to pass onto others in your honor. I am so thankful I had you. Even though it was brief, and not long enough; I am lucky to know you and your love. We will be together again I know.

When I was 15, my mother and I were in a car crash and a drunk driver killed my mom instantly. I wrote this page on her 65th birthday. She died two weeks after her 35th birthday. She was and always will be hands down the most amazing woman I have ever known. Everyone who knew her was always affected by her contagious energy and spirit and smile. We are all one of a kind, and she was just that kind of soul that you want to be around because you felt so good in her presence. What a gift. And I would gladly take the short 15 years I got to have with my mom and all the pain I went through when she died than to have had any other mom.

Take the time to tell the people you love that you love them. Say "I love you" as often as you can. Share what you love about them too, recognize how lucky you are to be in the physical presence of the wonderful people in your life. Life can change in an instant so don't take for granted the relationships that you have. Love freely and without reservation. Trust me, if you do that, I will guarantee by the end of your journey, you will be happy you did and have no regrets about it.

How did you get so lucky?

Self worth: have you ever found yourself wondering how some people seem so lucky? They seem to have it all, a great partner or if they're single, they are extremely happy to be, a dream home, the job, the family. They are surrounded by great friends. They have it all. Is that you? Or do you find yourself wondering how to get there?

A major contributing factor is self-worth. How do you see yourself; how do you view your worth? Do you feel that you are worth the best that life has to offer? Do you feel you are deserving of the greatest life you could have? Or do you feel like you don't deserve that? Like it's not in your cards to have that life?

This is the thing: we are all deserving of nothing but the best in this world and beyond. The best treatment from people, the best scenarios that lead to more best-case scenarios, the best energy around you, the best souls that help along the way, the best attraction to the best of anything you want.

It doesn't matter how you grew up or if people have always seemed to put you down. It doesn't matter if you have been hammered with the phrase that you "will never amount to anything"! This is up to you now. Let no one else's bad ideas become yours. Get past other people's negativity and create and draw into your universe a life of abundance, no one else can do it for you. And once you give credit to what you already have, you will notice the incredible things that begin to come your way. When you believe in yourself and what you know you deserve deep down, you will begin to accept the many blessings and wonderful advantages that will become your world. How we view ourselves basically creates how others will tune into and view us. In turn, what and how we experience life will be a direct reflection of that. It all comes back around to our feelings of our self worth. So, consider yourself one of the lucky ones who have an abundance of what ever it is that you desire and love and be so happy to live that life you deserve.

♡

Have you complimented yourself lately?

Be nice to yourself. When was the last time you gave yourself a compliment? Have you been kind to yourself lately? Ever?

Well, you need to be awesome to yourself. Right now, think of something you like about yourself. There's no right or wrong answer here. It could be anything you think of. Physical, mental, spiritual, or emotional. Maybe it was the way you handled a situation or how you dealt with someone or something, your health you're happy about, the way your family is getting along and what you contribute, maybe you give your time volunteering. The home you have created, the safe space for yourself, family, and friends. A work of art or a project you are proud of. Getting outside for a walk, sending a nice note to someone, or noting the way you laugh, anything.

Just take a bit of time every day and thank yourself for being you. Your quirky, lovable, self. We all have good and bad in us, as we are real, three-dimensional beings. But there is only one you, exactly you, love you, compliment you, cherish you, be your own best friend, your own hero, your own biggest cheerleader before anyone else's. Be kind to you!

Are you appreciating the effort you put into life?

Accomplishments! Big ones, little ones, we have all accomplished things. Do you take the time and realize your victories often? Give yourself some credit.... take a minute and think about your achievements.

Are you someone that doesn't recognize your own achievements unless others do? Do you think it's only important or it only matters if other people see it? Do you define yourself by your successes? Or are you lacking in giving yourself enough credit or any credit at all for the things you have accomplished?

Slow down, take a moment, and think back on something that you worked for and got the results from that you intended and wanted to get. Appreciate all your efforts and the energy you put behind something you wanted. Do not ever take for granted your hard work that turned into a success.

Are you holding back what makes you special?

Hey! Be thankful for the gifts you have, your specialties. Those things that only you have and can offer the world. Don't wait for some stranger to tell you what you're gifted at, because deep down you already know!

Take some inventory on yourself, on the things that make you stand out and apart from everyone else. Now own that! Nurture those parts of you-

Realize what you have to offer and explore and grow yourself. Begin to give freely without any expectation or return investment. Let everyone know who you are, subtly, loudly, however you feel; anyway, you want to share who you are. Please share without any shame or blame. Be proud of yourself. Don't hide away what the world around you needs. Whether you see it or not, others will love you for it!

In my life, I am surrounded by the most unique and interesting souls. I find so much joy in discovering new and interesting things in this world and especially in the people that surround me. I think it is so important to share who you really are, just being yourself. You end up with the most dynamic individuals around you that always make life interesting.

Do you realize how important the attitude you start the day with is?

Notice today how much your interactions and situations with others reflects upon your attitude. Did you start today happy, excited, and looking forward to life's daily adventures? Or did you wake up and groan in disappointment of the anticipation of another brutal day ahead that you expect is going to suck?

Now notice, how has your day been going so far.

Our thoughts and feelings really do create our experiences. That's why for some people life seems so hard and for others it's the most enjoyable experience. It will always come back to how we see things, how we look at things, how we feel first even before any moments happen.

Practice with your positive thoughts as soon as you wake up. Whether you are dreading your day ahead or worried about it, begin to change that initial behavior to believing that today is going to be great no matter what. And even if it has bumps in the road this great day, that is okay! You will still be okay! Practise positive thinking before your feet even hit the floor. Make it the first thing you do tomorrow and the day after and the day after that. Call it meditation or the power of prayer or good vibrations, but whatever you do, everything is okay when you believe it's going to be okay to start with!

And remember you can reset your emotions at any time. Maybe some days we do wake up on the wrong side of the bed, but that doesn't mean we have to stay on it.

Have you said thank you yet today?

What are you thankful for right now? In this moment? Today, as you read this. Close your eyes and take a couple deep breaths, taking as much time as you want and need, listening to your heart and soul.

Next say it out loud or silently a prayer of thanks and gratitude. To whom or whatever higher power you believe in, say you are grateful. That voice you talk to in your head, or heart tell that voice in your voice you are thankful.

Maybe it's God, Jesus, Buddha, angels, a tree, Mother Nature, the Universe, loved ones that have passed over the rainbow to the other side. Just say it. I am thankful because....... I am thankful for.......... .

Realize that no matter what may be missing in your world that there are always more great other things in it right now. The more you realize your abundance the more abundant you become. And then you realize you may have always been so. THANK YOU, THANK YOU, THANK YOU.

What do you celebrate?

Happy birthday! Happy anniversary! Happy whatever you want! Happy Hanukah! Dates to remember, the yearly celebrations and reminders of time.

D-day, V-day, Remembrance Day, Christmas, New Years, Valentines, St. Patrick's, Mother's, Father's, same day every year. Reoccurring and for a very good reason. To celebrate and reflect and appreciate the people, the moments, the journey of life.

I once dated someone that never knew even their own parents' birthdays. Never mind siblings or our anniversary. This had not occurred to me to be possible in a human being. And to this followed our first big argument. Their side was, "It's just a date, on a calendar, so what?" How ridiculous I thought, this person is unconscionable.

We need to celebrate these moments that we call upon every year. They are accomplishments. It's like a trophy of making it another year, recognizing our past. Recognizing our future. Respecting the dates that make our lives what they are. Celebrate as many people and moments as you possibly can. Make stuff up to be a cause to celebrate! This is part of the enjoyment of being alive!! Even the events in our lives that mark hardships and heartbreaks, when those days come around and remind us of our losses it is also a time of reflection. Another year you have made it on your journey and survived the painfulness of life without someone we love and miss. But you did get through. That is an accomplishment in itself. Celebrate everything you can, as much as you can. Recognize all that makes you who you are and all it has taken to be here.

Is it time for a toast?

Yes! Make a toast every chance you get.

You can put your fear of public speaking behind you, lift your glass and cheers. Cheers to anything and everything. Don't be shy and waste the perfect opportunity to put some gratitude and positive, happy, loving acknowledgment on someone or something. Just do it!

The more often you celebrate and toast to the small and the big stuff, the more stuff the universe will give you to celebrate.

Whenever my family sits together, we do a cheers and a toast. A kind gesture to the life and love we share together.

So, clink, clink, clink, clink! It's good fun and important to always celebrate, even on the most mundane of days, there will always be something to toast to.

What makes you feel like you are home?

Home. Home is a lot more than bricks and mortar. Have you ever thought about when your heart feels full, that feeling of the realization you are home within yourself?

Home can be the feeling you have when you are surrounded by certain people, or when everything feels complete and right and full of love. Maybe it's a moment when you pause, take a deep breath, and take in the beautiful view that surrounds you.

You feel like you are home when you smell baking in the oven, or comfort food on the stove. It could be the smell of coffee in the morning that was made for you by someone else.

Home is a safe, amazing space in our hearts and soul. There is a physical home but it's really the feeling inside that makes it a home. The people, memories, ease, love, forgiveness within it; this creates the feeling of being home and having a happy place.

Where is your happy place?

Do you have a happy place?

I like to think of it as a place where all my six senses are fulfilled at the same time. Visually, it is beautiful, smells amazing, and the sounds are wonderful. I can taste contentment and feel unbelievably grateful and happy, untouchable by anything negative. It is the most important place to be.

You can find yourself physically in your happy place, but you can also transport yourself there in your mind too. It's always with you. It can be imagined anytime you want to.

If it isn't often that you are in your happy places practice creating them in your mind and heart. Then you can go there and attract even more of these beautiful feelings through meditation. Just like the feeling of coming home, your happy place is the same idea.

You can take the feeling with you in your heart and carry it throughout all the amazing moments in your life and feel it over and over again. In tougher times, remind yourself of the feeling of being home and remind yourself what made you feel that way. That comfort, that contentment, that love.

For me it was and still is my grandma's house. She was the least judgmental person I have ever known. She always had my favorite food made, and there was such a comfort in her home that to this day I still can think about and feel in my heart. I always felt safe there. I find myself feeling the same contentment often when all feels right and easy in my world. Usually on a holiday or during special moments when we slow down and really take in all the wonderful enjoyments we are witnessing. Everyone is different and each of us feels things differently, just realize you can go back and remind yourself of times of feeling like you are home at any given moment.

Life is precious. Whether you are sick of it, happy with it or anywhere in between, life is a gift, and do you remember this?

The pure miracle that must first take place when each of us are conceived in itself is unbelievable. The odds and circumstances that must all come together perfectly at the perfect moment.

We definitely don't choose everything that happens to us, but we can do our best to influence our chances and results. I don't know how much of this in the end we do really control but we do control our attitudes. We do control our perspectives and both of those alter our experiences here.

When someone passes away too young it has a much different, much more profound affect on people. We say things like, "They were too young. They just started to live their lives; this is horrible." And it is. It is because time was taken away too fast, and we know that and recognize what a tragedy that is. When an old person goes, it's not with less love or sadness but there is a comfort in knowing they had the time. The time to live, to do, we say, "They had a good life, a long life, they got to live it."

We all want more time. It's the only thing we can't manufacture or buy. It isn't negotiable. It just is. And when it's over, we're all reminded to think about how and what we did with it. It makes us have to wonder about it, even if just for a moment. Life is precious, enjoy every moment.

Your Thoughts ... ♡

FIVE

Your Soul Was Meant to Shine Forever: Trusting the Universe and Have Faith

DEALING WITH ISSUES OF FAITH AS YOU RECOGNIZE THE PEOPLE MEANT TO BE IN YOUR LIFE

Have you ever met someone and known instantly that they had some purpose in your life?

Some call the chance meetings coincidence and others don't believe in coincidence or fate. I definitely believe in coincidence and in destiny and in fate. I've heard a person tell me that they believed that they made promises before they came to earth, before they were born here, promises to take care of certain soul mates. There are far too many factors sometimes that must all align for certain meetings with certain soul mates. So many in fact that there is no way we control these special encounters. It seems as though they were predestined or meant to be without us knowing it was even going to happen.

Maybe someone that's watching out for us puts the right person on our path at the right time for a reason. At one of my tougher moments in life, I prayed that God would please help me or send me an angel to help me. Then I prayed that I would recognize and know they were there for me when they showed up. Because the truth is that there could have already been people there for me that I didn't even realize were there to help me, so I shifted my prayers to helping me to recognize if there was someone put in my path to shine a light on me. Someone did show up and I did realize very quickly they were put in my path that day for a reason. This was the hope and guidance that I needed and prayed for. I will never forget what that kind, wise soul did for me and my life. That moment has forever changed me for the better for the rest of my life. I am grateful every day for the divine intervention. This person was put in my way to get me back on track to my soul purpose, and it worked!

The funny thing was that it had been about three weeks of unexpected circumstances that led me to be where I was that particular day. It was such a chance encounter, and the crazy thing was that it felt like I had known this person forever. They felt so comfortable and familiar, we were exactly on the same wavelength at that moment in time. I was in a position to listen, and they were in a position to listen. It took my life into a completely new place and renewed my self worth to this day. I am forever thankful. In a city with over a million people we found each other. Chance? Coincidence? Fate?

Did you know the universe is sometimes trying to send you a message?

Pay attention to the signs that the universe sends to you.

Have you ever seen a symbol or sign show up again and again?

For many years, I have always noticed things show up for me in the shape of a heart. Whether I'm cutting vegetables or driving through the mountains, I might see heart-shape in the rocks, clouds in the sky, or maybe someone is sending an emoji at the time I may need love more. Maybe for some, it's an animal that crosses your path and reminds you of a loved one. Or is there maybe to remind you simply of life's beauty. We are loved. Praying for a sign is one thing, praying we notice that sign is another. The universe could be putting all kinds of things you ask for in front of you, so slow down, pay attention, or you might just miss them! Eyes, and heart and soul open.

Do you think about how you can affect someone's day?

As much as we need good people in our lives have you taken much time to think about the roles that you play in other people's lives? What if destiny was also at work putting you in the path of others for reasons you don't yet know, maybe never will?

It could be just a simple smile you give to a stranger as easy as that and that might completely change their day. Maybe a passing conversation that to you isn't much of anything, but perhaps is profound to another. Maybe it's something the other person has been needing to hear.

Everyday our energy and thoughts are transforming not just ourselves but the people we are with, pass by, or love. Maybe someone we didn't even notice. We are constantly exchanging energy with one another in life, every time you encounter another person, we are unconsciously exchanging energy. An example of this is when you can feel a vibe from someone. It's the same thing. So, keep this in mind. It's easy to be polite. It's easy to smile. It's easy to just love.

Is your past controlling your future?

We are such the product of our parents, our families, our upbringing, our environment and our circumstances as we grew up. The environment in which we were raised stays within us forever. The good, the bad, the ugly, and everything in between.

So, what do we do when we decide that we can't allow any of the pain or ugly to dictate who we are or the rest of our lives? You simply can't erase it. It's not possible to unsee what you have already seen.

The truth is this: the things that we know weren't right or okay do not have the power to dictate who we are. Only we have the power to allow them to. Now, you can use these less than favorable moments to propel you and push you to let them work to your benefit in life. Or you can wallow in them and use them as excuses as to why things continue to go wrong and not work for you. The choice is always there, and you are the only one making it. You decide how you want to deal with your past.

Deep down inside, you know who you are, who you're meant to be, who you see you can be. Everything you have lived is a part of you, a part of your experiences. You may not like certain things, but that's also part of life. You need to be challenged and experience discomfort. That's what makes us grow.

Forgive. Love. Remember that everyone did the best they could whether you get it or like it or not. Family is the first, biggest, and perhaps most important teachers on forgiveness and moving forward, and especially gratitude we will ever have. Be thankful for whatever gifts—good, bad, and ugly—yours have given you. Learn from all of it.

Maybe someone hurt you, and it was left unresolved, no closure and it completely changed and effected you. It took over who you were and now you have become it. Have you allowed a situation or fear or other people to define you? It may be a part of what made you and your history but that is not all of who you are. You are also a product of your choices, your decisions.

When you got hurt in the past, leave it there. Stop there. Don't let it keep hurting and victimizing you day after day, month after month, year after year. It has probably already done enough damage to you so stop allowing it to take away the beauty of now! Start to let it go. Forgive yourself, decide to be better, forgive them even if they don't deserve it. Don't let that pain define you; remember, what you choose now creates your future. And you are the only one with the power to decide to move forward no one else can control that.

Being ashamed of something from your past should be acknowledged.

Maybe there is something you did or didn't do. Maybe it's something that was done to you by another person.

Keeping these things in the forefront of your mind means you are taking up space that could instead be used on healing the wounds of the past. The space needed to do the work to move forward and on. Staying stagnant in your pain is poison. Everyday like the hamster on the wheel: again, and again reliving agony makes no sense. Feeling ashamed and punishing yourself for something you can't change doesn't make any sense. It will never make the past any different, no matter how long you decide to torture yourself for it.

These are your lessons that need conquering. Your heart needs healing, and space to allow the light back in. your past is a part of who you are, PART, not all of who you are. Make it into the lesson it needs to be. Learn from it what there is to take from it. Know what you would do different or change for future reference. And work hard at letting it go. Forgive. You are worth it.

Do you know how powerful sending a future note to yourself can be?

A couple of months ago, I was checking my daily calendar on my phone for the following day. Just double checking in advance so I had a good idea of what tomorrow was looking like, and this was when I saw it. I saw something that I didn't recall adding. It read:

"Today your life will be better than 1 year ago!"

This made me cry. It made me cry for many reasons. It meant that the year before, I went into my calendar and added this for future me. It was a reminder to myself of all the pain I was going through at that exact moment; that in a year it would without a doubt be better. What a gift to receive. What a gift to myself.

The year I entered my message to future me, I was going through intense cancer treatment and about to undergo a week of internal radiation. About to be bedridden on my back without any movement at all, radiation buzzing on my internal organs every hour on the hour twenty-four hours a day. I knew then life would only get better, and it has completely done a

360-degree turn for the best. I am happy to say, I feel amazing probably the best in my life, mentally, spiritually, emotionally, physically is always a work in progress(lol)! And I have been in remission now going into my second year!

Now it's your turn- send yourself a note, or a love letter to your future self with positive vibes and messages, date it with a reminder and put it on repeat for every year ahead into your virtual calendar or future day timer. We all carry around these devices that have calendars built into them, use them to your advantage, not just to be organized but to love yourself and remind yourself how beautiful you are and how beautiful life can be. Be kind to yourself and encouraging, good luck!

What would young you tell old you?

If you look back over the years and reflected on the times you worried and lost sleep over things, you might now see that in hindsight those things were never worth the wasted time and energy. Time has moved on and now you have probably forgotten many of the issues that caused those sleepless nights. So, what advice would present you right now tell your future self about stressing out over petty issues?

Try looking back even a few years ago or months ago. Knowing what you know now, what advice would you give to yourself? Would you tell yourself that things will work out fine or better than fine? Would you say that you are going to be okay, so stop stressing so much since there's no need to!?

Sometimes what we believe in the moment to be so important but is out of our reach or control we allow to take up so much space in ourselves. And the fact is, it doesn't need to be that way. Imagine your old worries gone as yesterday is gone.

Forgotten and gotten over. You've moved on from the stress, and you are still here! Still living and breathing and smarter than ever! Look back then and look at you now! Every thing is going to be alright!

There are very few things in life worth losing sleep over. And I know how it feels sometimes when it seems all is not well with the world, and it brings us down. But we must realize the importance of shaking off the feeling of being a victim or the lack of control we might be feeling. Get back to a happy focus or gratitude for other things that are good and get back to feeling okay. Everything is going to be just fine. Remember that no amount of worry changed any outcome.

Do you use meditation or prayer everyday for your positive intentions?

Every day, I pray. I pray that God, my angels, the universe, and all higher power than me; be with me today. Be with me and protect my loved ones and my family.

I ask for help with the things I feel I need to work on. Like shutting my mouth at the right time, listening more, and to please help me to use and say the right words that are needed or maybe important words for someone else to hear today.

I pray for guidance and to please put me in the right place at the right time with the right people and intentions. I ask God to put me to use for my greatest and best good.

I am not trying to preach about religion here or church. Everybody has their own belief system and is absolutely entitled to that. This is part of what makes us so dynamic. There is no judgment from me on this, I just believe what I believe and my relationship with my spiritual side is my belief system. What ever your thoughts are about God, Buddha, any type of divine being, aliens, angels, the universe, or nothing at all, it's your personal choice and no one has any right to tell you, you are wrong. And, by all means, our beliefs or lack thereof does not make us any less lovable! I have best friends who have all thoughts about spirituality and creation. All faiths, and some with no faiths. I am not here on this planet to judge anyone especially on something so personal as their beliefs. The truest thing I know is that kindness and love are more important than anything we can be or do.

I trust. I believe and I trust that the universe is working with me, creating the way and the path that I am meant to travel. I am right now where I am meant to be in this moment. I may not always understand why or whether I get it or not, or why I may end up in certain places or situations. I must understand that we are not in control of everything. I believe there are higher powers at work behind the scenes making things happen in synchronicity that may only become obvious to us later on in life, in hindsight. We choose what we do with what we are given. I do try my best to manifest the best feelings in life I can. To daily take the time to breathe, reflect, be thankful, mindful, and to create and pray is so important to our mental and emotional selves. I personally have had many fallings out with my spiritual side, and in the end when I have found my way back to believing in something bigger than what we just see in front of us. I see now that my life always becomes better and more blessed. This is what works for me, I am always a better person when I have faith working for me in my life.

Did you know there is no such thing as wasted time?

I bet you can pinpoint in your life when you thought you wasted time. Wasted time in a relationship with the wrong person. Wasted time at a thankless job for too long. Wasted time being lazy and unproductive. It's probably pretty easy to look back and see many situations we took too long to change.

But was it really wasted time, or was it that you just weren't ready? Maybe you lacked the tools needed to move on at that particular moment in time. Perhaps there was still more to learn from those moments in time before you could make a move.

Instead of blaming yourself for wasting so much time, try embracing this time in your life. You can't go back and change the past, but you can search for meaning in it. If you right now find yourself stuck, figure out what you want instead of this. And it all begins with a thought! The realization that it's time to go, move on, and then the thoughts of what positive future comes next. What would you like your life to look like after this?

What are you going to do today to change tomorrow?

Whether you are feeling sad, lazy, sick and tired, on autopilot, let down, or maybe you are happy, content, excited. No matter how you find yourself right now, begin to put an effort into something that will result in conquering a better tomorrow.

You may have to force yourself to do the extra bit of work, or it may come easily. But just get off your butt and do it. Whatever it may be, a positive shift to get the momentum going.

Exercising as dreadful as it may seem to some people is like free drugs that are so good for your mind and body. Once you begin a physical outlet for your emotions, and to build up your confidence you will want to keep it going. The hardest part is getting there, the work out is the easy part. Just start. Walk outside everyday if you don't do gyms. Take a yoga class, hit class, join a learn how to run group. Take up golf. Just start! And begin your day with a quick affirmation and tell yourself how much better you will feel afterwards. And physical activity is just one idea of what you can do today to change tomorrow.

Try saving the latte money you spend everyday and put it in a jar. Begin saving money for that trip or car, or whatever fund. Talk to someone. Call an old friend that you haven't connected with in a while, reach out.

Just put an effort into something you want to improve on. You don't need to announce it to anyone-it's usually better if you don't. This is just between you and yourself for your tomorrow. And don't forget to smile!

How do you know when the universe is taking care of you?

When I had my first chemotherapy treatment as I was going through cancer, it was no coincidence, the seat I was sat in for the next 4.5 hours. The universe had a plan.

I struggled so much with my diagnoses that my doctors had prescribed me a heavy anti-anxiety medication to be taken every 3 hours, every day. My diagnosis and treatments were one of the most traumatic times I have ever been through.

Chemotherapy round one, scary, unbelievable, and surreal to find myself here. Sitting across from me, though, all tied up just like me with tubes and chemicals and beeping machines was a young man. Very professionally dressed, business casual. He was with a young professional-looking woman as his chemo buddy. They looked like they knew the ropes. They sat fearlessly across from me. As I watched them during this time, I saw laughter, smiles, time well spent together by the way they acted. Watching them calmed me. It made me feel good to see smiles in such dark places and dark moments. They still managed to be happy in the moment. And that was all I needed to see, to remember to keep smiling, and to know it is all going to be okay. I still think back to this because it was a turning point for me. It reminded me to find the light in the dark, because it is there; sometimes it's just tougher to see.

Are you living in the moment?

This exact moment in time you will never have again. You will never be able to go back and repeat these circumstances ever again.

The place you are at in your mind, and heart and soul, the health you are in, the people around you and the age you are, and they all are.

You can physically return to almost anywhere you have been before as far as location goes, but never again will it ever be as it is right now.

Enjoy the moment. Pay attention to the little things that make it so special. And feel it. Feel the moments in the present, engage in your surroundings. Relax and let things go for now, everything else can wait.

Most people have an online presence, so how present are you online?

The art of illusion. We live in a time of everyone knowing everything about our lives if we let them. Do you spend more time there than in the present moment taking place around you?

Besides the time commitment, our online lives tend to be only the best photos, or funniest and most epic times. And that is just the nature of the beast. But remember that everyone out there is doing the same. It is a great representation maybe but, really, it's the creation of an illusion. An illusion in the sense that you can only see what the magician wants you to see. The projection of the best life people are living.

It's wonderful to see others happy. It can actually make your own day better to see joy in other people's worlds, maybe living vicariously through them for a moment. Or not. If you are not in a good place yourself than this might make it seem worse.

So, remember not to get caught up in comparing your life to others. Take it with a grain of salt. Think about your own account and what you choose and how you decide what to post and talk about.

Take a step back every now and then and rejoin the land of the living. Put your electronics away, not just down, away in a drawer where you can't see or hear them for an hour at least a day. Take a break. And remember that it is all the art of illusion in its simplest form.

Are you near-sighted or far-sighted?

I realized on a road trip as we drove through the mountains that when I focused only on my immediate surroundings that I lost focus on the background.

I was looking so hard for wildlife and as my eyes were searching nearby only, I was missing out on all the beautiful scenery all around us.

Life can be that way and reflect that analogy perfectly. When we focus so much on one area or thing, we can lose sight of the bigger picture. All the beauty that surrounds us is just as important as the one thing that we may be focusing too much of our energy and sight on. Keep your eyes open and take in all the views.

Have you ever had something show up at the perfect moment that you needed it?

The power of an energy bigger than that of any human and ourselves is watching over us, this I am definitely convinced of.

I have many examples of this personally, but here's one I am going to share right now....

I woke up today after a very restless sleep. My night was sleepless due to an argument that was very emotional I had the night before. Every time in the night I woke up, I kept telling myself that I don't want to feel these emotions anymore. I want to move forward; I am tired of feeling this yuckiness. But it wasn't going away.

As the night left me and morning crept in, I decided that day I would be in the moment. I'd let the last days events dissolve and focus on right now, what is in front of me. And my moment was to feel happy. I let go of what is gone and I was happy.

As I opened my journal that I was using to write this book, and it flipped to a page already written on randomly in the middle of my book. It happened to have the same, exact date but two years earlier. An entry I wrote exactly two years to the day.

Where I was on this exact day two years before was waiting at the Cross Cancer Institute to learn what degree, what stage my cancer was at. We already knew I had the disease, but just not how much it had spread. It was one of the scariest times of my life that moment. Having no clue if I was to experience the chance to get to watch my kids grow up or another Christmas with my family. The chance to grow old. The fear of leaving my husband and kids behind so young. They would have to live without me, just as I had lived without my mom. I was terrified of the information that was about to be handed to me.

And today, right now in this moment, two years later, I am writing this as a survivor! I am on the other side of it. I prayed so hard to one day be where I am right now. Where I am today. I am here. I will not waste anymore of my precious time, beautiful time, feeling dragged down and focused on the past, the things that are out of reach and gone. I can control myself. I can choose love. Talk about perfect timing. Talk about a reminder of how precious life is in the exact moment I needed it. What an example of coincidence or sacred intervention or whatever you call it, but it was quite the chance of opening up to that exact page that exact moment in time. Thank you, God, Buddha, all my angels, the universe for your perfect gift of timing and the amazing gift of life you graciously reminded me of.

Who do you consider your chosen family?

"No man is a failure who has friends," wrote Clarence Angel second class. This was the inscription he wrote in the book *Tom Sawyer* that Clarence gave to George Bailey in Frank Capra's *It's a Wonderful Life.*

We need friends. Period. There may be times we are surrounded by people but are they true friends? There are many degrees of friendships and acquaintances. But real close friendships, the ones you trust, and you believe in.The kind that your friends believe in you, accept you, love you.

We need people in our lives that put a smile on our face when we think about them. We need people we can laugh with, share with, support and to support us.

Think about those precious relationships that make you smile. Now think about the last time you saw them or spent time together. These are the souls we need to be with as much as possible. These are the souls that when we are together our hearts feel lighter and our spirits seem to be dancing.

You are the company you keep. Think about how you feel after you spend time with your closest friends. Now think about who you spend the most time with.

The company you keep mirrors who you are. The people we spend the most time with reflects ourselves.

If you don't like what you see around, you then should ask yourself what are you doing there? It might be better to be alone too if you aren't with the right people.

We can be around people that feel good to be around. They bring out excitement, wonder, happiness, and good things in life. A cup of warm milk that warms our souls. People we admire for one or many reasons and inspire us.

Like attracts like.

Look at who you surround yourself with.

Your vibe attracts your tribe!

It is also true that sometimes relationships can be like a rubber band or boomerang, they stretch out and go a distance but return and snap back. This is the natural ebbs and flows of relationships. We aren't always in the same head or heart space at the same time, so there are times when friendships circle back around after distancing. And there are the ones that never circle back around and we are very okay with that too!

Don't ever take for granted the friends you have. Take advantage of the wonderful gift that they are and what a gift your relationship is.

In my life my blood family wasn't always a place of comfort for me. We went through so much pain and heartache together that eventually it took its toll on our relationships for a certain period of time. I needed my friends more than ever. This is when I really realized the feeling of having a family out of the people around me, who I choose to be with. We can create our own family that is not made up of the same DNA. People we are not born into but feel like we were. One of life's greatest blessings are our friends. Our chosen family.

What makes you memorable?

Isn't it interesting that when people pass over to the other side, how differently we then see them?

All the annoying habits about them that bothered people are now their funny or endearing qualities that we recognize were one of a kind. The wacky things that now we are going to talk about and miss for the rest of our lives. Or maybe not. But we do have a hole where the people we loved used to be once they are gone. A space not possible to fill with anyone else. Their own unique space in our hearts.

We are funny creatures. So much knowledge comes from hindsight. Pay attention to the things that maybe drive you crazy about people you love and remember they are only human too, and what if suddenly they weren't doing those things anymore that irritate you. I bet you would miss it. What would people miss about you the most? Does that answer make you want to change anything? Make you want to do things a bit differently or not?

Your Thoughts ... ♡

SIX

Summary

Life sure is interesting. It can be so full of light. It can be so dark at times.

We are all connected. Each of us carries within our soul star dust, the same little sparkle of light in each of us from the same beautiful source of love that we came from, and ultimately will return to. Eventually, we all make our journeys back home.

We all need to feel love, kindness, and a sense of belonging. And sometimes we don't get that from others, so we must learn to give it to ourselves. Learn to love yourself, forgive yourself, be patient with yourself, be kind to yourself. It is only in our own self care that we then can move on and practice giving back to others what we most need.

Practice living life one day at a time. When things feel so heavy, remind yourself at that exact moment what you have power over. You have power over how you feel, and how you act, right now. Yesterday is gone, tomorrow isn't here either, but right now in front of us is what we do have. What can you do right now, in this moment to make life the best it can be? What can you do today to set up a better tomorrow?

Whatever makes you feel good in life, those things that bring your soul joy and feed your happiness and inner spirit, do them over and over and over again. The things or feelings you get when your heart is full and singing, recreate whatever that is again and again as often as you can. Try to start each day thinking about the wonderful moments in life and begin each day with excitement of what is yet to come. Choose to feel happy.

Love without fear or judgement. Tell people you love them. Don't take your family or friendships for granted. Cherish them. Don't let anger or situations from the past interfere with the potential of the present. If things need mending or fixing, then do your best to fix them. That will require some true soul-searching and self-reflection, but the intention to make something better will never be a waste of time, no matter the outcome. Sometimes, we just need to move on with or without an apology for the sake of our own sanity. Choose to forgive.

Be open minded. Consider all possibilities. Detach from any outcome and try to realize the potential in every situation. Remember to ask yourself in tougher moments, what can I learn from this and how can I grow from this? If we can find purpose or opportunity in the challenges, then we are on our way to where we need to go. Leading you to ultimately exactly where you are meant to be. This is when synchronicity and serendipity and coincidence all begin to show up!

If through all my toughest times and lessons I've learned, if going through all this good, bad, and the ugly can even help just one person then it was all worth it. By accepting ourselves first and then each other, and realizing that we are all human just out there doing the best we know how to, wouldn't life be so much kinder? Simplify things, get rid of the drama. We should be loving each other, especially in the times where you really aren't feeling it. Push yourself to be and do better. You might not have the power to go back and change things from the past, but you do have the power to change how you feel about them now.

You are one of a kind. Your experiences and how they affected you and molded you are unique to you. There is no one else in the universe the same as you. We connect through similarity, polarity, and understanding. Like attracts like. I know it's a cliché, but it is also true. We are magnets of energy. The moment you stop comparing yourself to others is the moment you can let your true spirit soar, and your light shine. Be who you are, and be what you want to be. Shit will always happen in life; it does not define us but challenges us, sometimes to our core. Have faith, never give up hope. Your light, your energy is so precious you have to share it. Let people know you and love you. Give yourself the permission and the freedom to just be you!

Afterword

I hope you enjoyed my words and thoughts. With every cell in my body, heart and soul I wish you love, forgiveness, breath, light, and adventure. May you always find peace and comfort and feelings of contentment living out each day to its fullest. Be kind to yourself.

Remember that even in the darkest moments there is always a pilot light glowing on even if the flames are out; and that is the light of the divine living in everyone of us. In each of our souls is the light that connects us to one another in this world and beyond. Honor your light, the light in your beautiful soul.

Love, Mandi

I've been alone
I've been together
I've been apart
I've been broken
I've been loved
I've been forgiven
I've been alive
I've been me

Acknowledgments

I want to give a shout out to my amazing family. I have the most wonderful immediate and extended family a girl could ask for. So many wonderful times and memories we make, enjoying life to its fullest. I love you guys.

Thank you to my army of soul mates I share my life with, my friends. You are what helps keep me sane, and I am so lucky to be surrounded by the coolest people ever!! Cheers!

About the Author

Mandi Miller has mastered the art of finding light even in the darkest of places. A self-proclaimed soul searcher, lover of life and fun, she has a passion for living in the moment and is a huge fan of forgiveness.

She lives outside of Edmonton, Alberta, Canada with her husband, two kids, Great Dane Stella and old lady black cat Misses Ming Ming.

Visit Mandi at: www.indyroxstar.com

Manufactured by Amazon.ca
Bolton, ON